ABCs of Serging

Other books available from Krause

Robbie Fanning, Series Editor

Contemporary Quilting Series

Contemporary Quilting Techniques: A Modular Approach, by Patricia Cairns

Fast Patch: A Treasury of Strip-Quilt Projects, by Anita Hallock

Fourteen Easy Baby Quilts, by Margaret Dittman

Machine-Quilted Jackets, Vests, and Coats, by Nancy Moore

The Quilter's Guide to Rotary Cutting, by Donna Poster

Scrap Quilts Using Fast Patch, by Anita Hallock

Speed-Cut Quilts, by Donna Poster

Are you interested in a quarterly newsletter about creative uses of the sewing machine, serger, and knitting machine? Write to The Creative Machine-ABC, PO Box 2634, Menlo Park, CA 94026.

Creative Machine Arts Series

The Button Lover's Book, by Marilyn V. Green

Claire Shaeffer's Fabric Sewing Guide

The Complete Book of Machine Embroidery, by Robbie and Tony Fanning

Creative Nurseries Illustrated, by Debra Terry and Juli Plooster

Creative Serging Illustrated, by Pati Palmer, Gail Brown, and Sue Green

Distinctive Serger Gifts and Crafts, by Naomi Baker and Tammy Young

The Expectant Mother's Wardrobe Planner, by Rebecca Dumlao

The Fabric Lover's Scrapbook, by Margaret Dittman

Friendship Quilts by Hand and Machine, by Carolyn Vosburg Hall

Innovative Serging, by Gail Brown and Tammy Young

Innovative Sewing, by Gail Brown and Tammy Young

Owner's Guide to Sewing Machines, Sergers, and Knitting Machines, by Gale Grigg Hazen

Petite Pizzazz, by Barb Griffin

Putting on the Glitz, by Sandra L. Hatch and Ann Boyce

Sew, Serge, Press, by Jan Saunders

Sewing and Collecting Vintage Fashions, by Eileen MacIntosh

Simply Serge Any Fabric, by Naomi Baker and Tammy Young

Twenty Easy Machine-Made Rugs, by Jackie Dodson

Know Your Sewing Machine Series, by Jackie Dodson

Know Your Bernina, second edition

Know Your Brother, with Jane Warnick

Know Your Elna, with Carol Ahles

Know Your New Home, with Judi Cull and Vicki Lyn Hastings

Know Your Pfaff, with Audrey Griese

Know Your Sewing Machine

Know Your Singer

Know Your Viking, with Jan Saunders

Know Your Serger Series, by Naomi Baker and Tammy Young

Know Your baby lock

Know Your Pfaff Hobbylock

Know Your White Superlock

Teach Yourself to Sew Better Series, by Jan Saunders

A Step-by-Step Guide to Your Bernina

A Step-by-Step Guide to Your New Home Sewing Machine

A Step-by-Step Guide to Your Sewing Machine

A Step-by-Step Guide to Your Viking

ABCs of Serging

A Complete Guide to Serger Sewing Basics

Tammy Young and Lori Bottom

 **krause publications**

700 E. State Street • Iola, WI 54990-0001
Telephone: 715/445-2214

Published in Iola, Wisconsin, 54990 by
Krause Publications

Cover design by Anthony Jacobson
Designed by Martha Vercoutere
Illustrations by Chris Hansen

Manufactured in the United States of America

Library of Congress Cataloging in Publication Data

Young, Tammy

    ABCs of serging: a complete guide to Serger
sewing basics / Tammy Young and Lori Bottom.

    p. cm. — (Creative machine arts series)

Includes index.

ISBN 0-8019-8195-6

1. Serging. I. Bottom, Lori. II. Title. III.
Series.

TT713.Y68 1992	91-58294
646.2'044 - dc20	CIP

890 098

Contents

Foreword

by Naomi Baker

When teaching serging classes across the country, I usually take a quick survey of my students on how much they use their serger and how comfortable they are in using it. Unfortunately, most of them tell me they lack the confidence to make basic adjustments in serging, for fear of not being able to get it back to the "perfect stitch" or of putting the serger out of adjustment. They received the basics from their dealer when they purchased their serger, but after getting home, they were intimidated by the dials and levers.

As a result, that serger remains in the box or is used for little more than seam finishing. These students have repeatedly requested a book that teaches them the basics, so they can enjoy all the time-saving, professional finishing and decorative uses of that wonderful little machine.

Here is the book you requested! If you want to become more proficient in the use of your serger, *ABCs of Serging* is for you.

This book leads you through the basics of serging and will help you to overcome the fear of changing that dial, so you can move on to using your serger to its limits. Tammy and Lori give you step-by-step instructions with clear illustrations on basic techniques. You will learn threading and how to adjust tension, stitch width, and stitch length on your machine. After practicing the basics, you will make use of these techniques in rolled edge, flatlocking, decorative serging, and simple garment construction.

You will then find you are no longer intimidated by turning the tension dials.

As a bonus, this book includes time-saving and troubleshooting tips from the *National Serger Teachers Advisory Board,* a group of experts who have taught serger classes and are innovative in developing the newest in serger techniques.

I would like to invite you to use this book as your personal instructor, taking your time to develop your serging skills in your own home. Keep the *ABCs* near your serger so you can refer to it often. Following Tammy and Lori's instructions, practice each technique until you become experienced on your own serger and you can enjoy serging as much as I do.

Happy serging!

Preface

"I'm afraid to change thread." "I can't get the tension adjusted correctly." "Converting to a rolled edge is too complicated." "It's all so confusing!" We're constantly hearing how intimidating the serger is to someone who is just beginning to use one.

Even if you are a sewing whiz, the serger is an entirely different piece of equipment—with loopers, knives, and brand-new techniques to understand. So when Chilton series editor Robbie Fanning suggested a *basic* serging book, we jumped at the opportunity.

During the last ten years serger technology has advanced rapidly. At the same time, serger sewing enthusiasts have developed an incredible number of new techniques and decorative serging options. The current serger books on the market are either too advanced for the beginning serger user or else they don't reflect much of the new information.

Our challenge was to sort out the most important facts, apply them to every serger brand and model, and organize them in a logical, step-by-step format so that anyone could work smoothly through and learn to use the machine to its full potential.

We've packed a lot of information, skills, and techniques into this book as a foundation and future reference for your serging success. But don't stop here! Once you've mastered the basics, much more awaits: additional garment construction and advanced decorative techniques, home decorating projects, serger quilting, and heirloom serging. There's also much more to learn about serging specialty fabrics, and there are lots of gift, craft, and accessory ideas.

For additional inspiration, see Other Books by the Authors in the back of this book, or visit your local sewing machine dealer and fabric stores.

First, however, back to basics. Join us as we take you step by step through the ABCs of Serging.

Tammy Young
Lori Bottom

Acknowledgments

Without the help of seven well-known serger experts, this book would be much less informative. These experts were responsible not only for adding tips and ideas to the manuscript, but also for developing many of the skills and techniques presented: Naomi Baker, Gail Brown, Ronda Chaney, Sue Green-Baker, Gale Grigg Hazen, Jan Saunders, and Ruthann Spiegelhoff.

We call this talented group our **National Serger Teachers Advisory Board.** Their experience and accomplishments are listed on the following pages. We sincerely appreciate all their time, hard work, and encouragement.

A special thank you to Sue Green-Baker, who was one of the first innovators in serger sewing and has been active in the field ever since. Not only did she serve on our Advisory Board; she also helped with the initial concept and organization of this book.

Special thanks also to board members Naomi Baker (who was always available for extra consultation and moral support) and Gale Grigg Hazen (whose excellent tips, techniques, and suggestions would practically fill a separate book).

Another major thanks to our incomparable illustrator and friend, Chris Hansen. When not busy drawing, he's turning out creative projects on his serger.

And without our organized and knowledgeable editor, Robbie Fanning, this book wouldn't have been written. Thanks for encouraging us to go back to the beginning and write a basic book to help even more people learn the fun and excitement of serger sewing.

The following are registered trademark names used in this book: *baby lock, Designer Edge, Hobbylock, Seams Great,* and *Superlock.*

National Serger Teachers Advisory Board

Naomi Baker—Springfield, Oregon. Writer, classroom and seminar instructor, guest lecturer, and serger technique researcher. Formerly a cooperative extension agent, Palmer/Pletsch Serger Workshop instructor, and Stretch & Sew employee.

Education: Home economics graduate, Iowa State University.

Published Books: **Distinctive Serger Gifts & Crafts; Simply Serge Any Fabric; Know Your baby lock; Know Your White Superlock; Know Your Pfaff Hobbylock.**

Gail Brown—Hoquiam, Washington. Prolific writer, television personality, guest lecturer, and industry consultant. Formerly a fabric company marketing director, Stretch & Sew communications director, Palmer/Pletsch Serger Workshop instructor, and *Serger Update* and *Sewing Update* newsletter editor.

Education: Clothing and textiles graduate, University of Washington.

Published Books: **Instant Interiors; Quick Napkin Creations; Innovative Serging; Innovative Sewing; Creative Serging Illustrated; Creative Serging: The Complete Guide to Decorative Overlock Sewing; Sewing with Sergers; Sew a Beautiful Wedding; Sensational Silk; Super Sweater Idea Book.**

Ronda Chaney—Redwood City, California. Chair of Home Economics at Canada College, specializing in textiles and clothing. Sewing school instructor, guest lecturer, free-lance writer. Consultant for community fashion production programs and private clothing businesses.

Education: Bachelor of science degree in home economics and education, University of Missouri. Masters of science degree in home economics with an emphasis in textiles and clothing, San Francisco State University.

Sue Green-Baker—Benicia, California. Writer, highly experienced instructor, and technical expert. Formerly a sales manager for sewing machines and sergers at New York Fabrics (a large fabric-store chain), national education coordinator for Tacony (*baby lock* sergers), and Palmer/Pletsch Serger Workshop instructor and manager.

Published Books: ***Sewing with an Overlock; Creative Serging Illustrated.***

Gale Grigg Hazen—Saratoga, California. Owner of and instructor for The Sewing Place, a creative sewing school. Certified color and image consultant, writer, and guest lecturer. Formerly sold and repaired sergers, instructed at the San Francisco Sewing Workshop.

Published Books: ***Owner's Guide to Sewing Machines, Sergers, and Knitting Machines; Sew Sane: A Common Sense Approach to Making Your Sewing Machine Work for You.***

Jan Saunders—Dublin, Ohio. Writer, guest lecturer, and in-store instructor. Education director for Chilton Book Company "Sew Much Better" educational program. Formerly education director for a major sewing-machine company and a large fabric-store chain.

Education: New York Fashion Institute of Technology. Home economics, secondary education, and business graduate of Adrian College, Adrian, Michigan.

Published Books: ***A Step-by-Step Guide to Your Bernina; A Step-by-Step Guide to Your New Home Sewing Machine; A Step-by-Step Guide to Your Sewing Machine; A Step-by-Step Guide to Your Viking; Sew, Serge, Press; Know Your White; Know Your Viking; Illustrated Speed Sewing.***

About the Authors

Ruthann Spiegelhoff—Racine, Wisconsin. Fabric store owner and enthusiastic sewing instructor. Founder and owner of Great Copy Pattern Company. Twenty years of experience in the retail fabric business. Free-lance writer.

Education: Home economics graduate, Western Michigan University.

Tammy Young has combined creativity and practicality in her writing and publishing career. With a home economics degree from Oregon State University, she has an extensive background in the ready-to-wear fashion industry as well as being a former extension agent and high school home economics teacher. Tammy has co-authored seven other Chilton books.

Living and working in San Francisco's Marina District, Tammy founded and managed the *Sewing Update* and *Serger Update* newsletters before selling them in 1991. When her hectic schedule allows, she travels stateside and abroad, frequently picking up trends and ideas for her writing.

Lori Bottom is a free-lance writer and a lifelong sewing enthusiast. Fashion design, fashion merchandising, and textile science were her major areas of study at California Polytechnic State University, from which she graduated with a degree in home economics. Before free-lancing, Lori worked as a computer analyst, training coordinator, and on the *Update Newsletter* editorial staff.

An avid serger user, Lori enjoys sewing many projects for herself and others. She lives in San Anselmo, California, with her husband David Tanzer. Together they travel around the west in their small airplane.

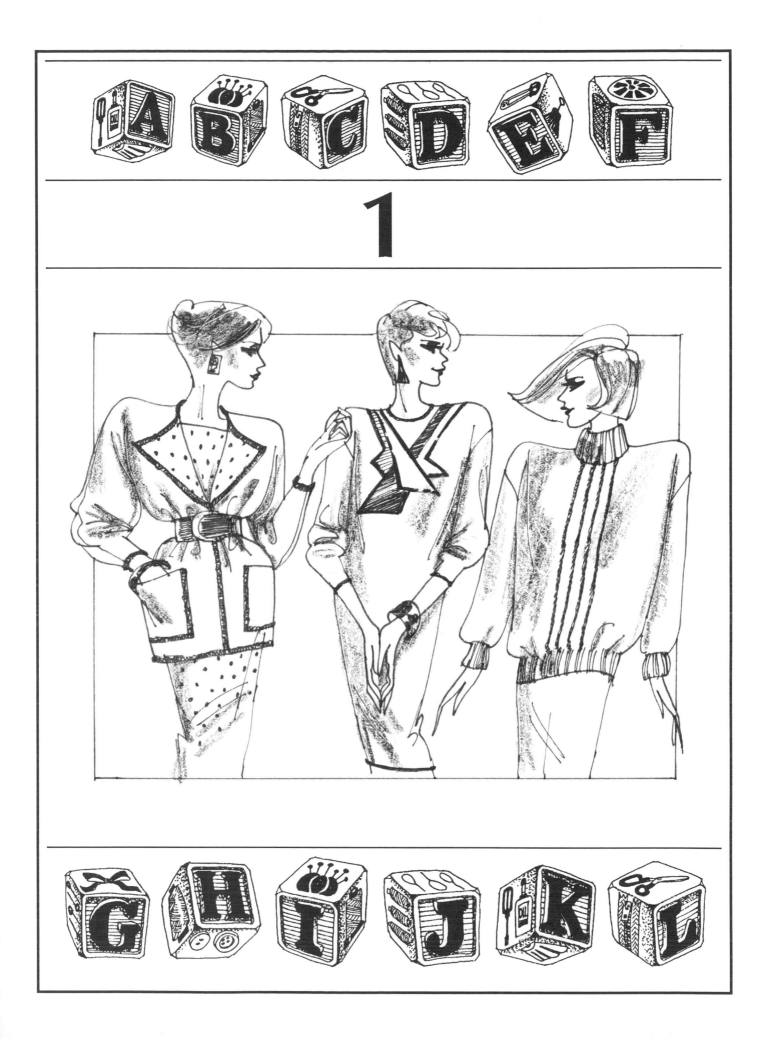

1

Anyone Will Love a Serger

✂ **A Serger? What's That?**
✂ **What Can a Serger Do for You?**
✂ **How to Use This Book**
✂ **Serger Shopping Guidelines**

A Serger? What's That?

If you're reading this book, either:

1. You already know what a serger is and want to learn more about this sewing phenomenon, or

2. You're saying, "What in the world is serging all about?" and are in for a pleasant surprise.

When discussing our hobby/profession, the most common question we receive from our nonsewing friends and acquaintances is, "A serger? What's that?"

Our usual response: "It's a special type of sewing machine that trims, stitches, and overcasts the edge at the same time. It makes the type of seams you see in T-shirts." We also explain that sergers are faster and more compact than conventional sewing machines. (Fig. 1-1)

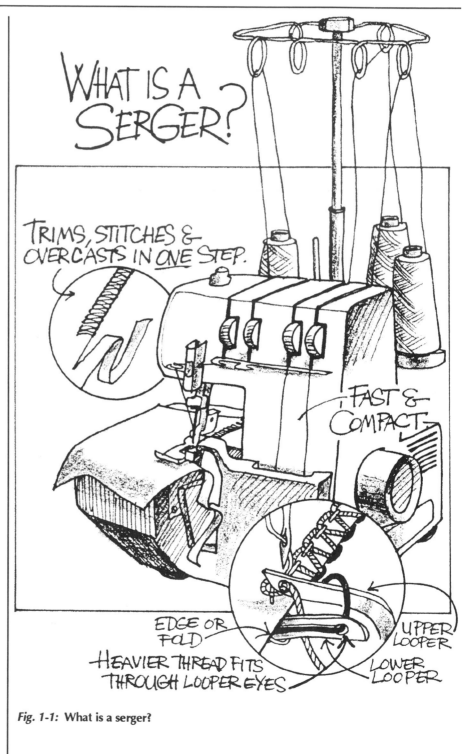

Fig. 1-1: What is a serger?

One major difference between a serger and a conventional sewing machine is that the serger uses *loopers* instead of a bobbin. Because the loopers are larger than a needle and do not pass through the fabric, they can be threaded with heavy decorative thread. But this also means that serging must be done on edges or folds.

> *It helps to think of the loopers acting like knitting needles, locking threads at the edge of the fabric and never needing to penetrate through it.*
> **Ronda Chaney**

Sergers (also called overlock machines) were first developed for the industrial market. They were large, loud, and offered the seamstress little protection from the exposed knives used for trimming the fabric edge.

In 1967, a Japanese company introduced the first home serger model, aimed at tailors, alteration shops, cottage industries, and people trained in professional factory methods. The popularity of home serging spread rapidly from Japan to the United States and other countries.

As more and more American women joined the work force, serger sewing offered them both the speed they needed to fit home sewing into their busy schedules and the professional-quality results they required for their career wardrobes.

Sergers have generated a renewal of interest and excitement in home sewing. Every major sewing machine company now markets overlock machines under its own brand name, and new serging techniques are being developed continually.

What Can a Serger Do for You?

Working side by side with your sewing machine, a serger will add greatly to your sewing options. While your sewing machine is important for top-stitching and edge-stitching, numerous tailoring and couture techniques, and a myriad of decorative stitch options, a serger will duplicate many factory techniques including:

✂ **Rolled edges**—For everything from napkins to chiffon, serged rolled edges (see Chapter 14) provide a neat, attractive finish on a single-layer edge or hem. (Fig. 1-2)

Fig. 1-2: **Rolled edges.**

✂ **Ravel-free seam finishing**—With your serger, you can finish allowances of straight-stitched seams or serge-seam and finish in one operation. Either way, your seam allowances will be neat, attractive, and ravel-free. (Fig. 1-3)

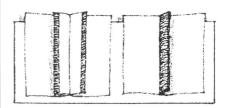
Fig. 1-3: **Ravel-free seam finishing.**

✂ **Stretch seaming**—You can quickly and durably serge knits, swimsuits, and aerobic wear. The built-in stretch of most serged stitching keeps the thread from breaking when a seam is stretched. (Fig. 1-4)

Fig. 1-4: **Stretch seaming.**

✂ Pucker-free sewing—With proper tension settings, no matter how narrow the seam or how delicate the fabric, serged stitches form evenly over the serger's stitch finger, preventing puckering. Lace, lingerie, and other difficult fabrics can be serged beautifully . (Fig. 1-5)

✂ Reversible options— Because serged stitching can be ornamental as well as practical, it can be used on the outside of a garment or for reversible garments. (Fig. 1-6)

Fig. 1-6: Reversible options.

✂ Even feeding—Two layers of fabric will feed evenly through the serger, making it easy to match stripes or other patterned fabric. You won't need to worry about one layer slipping. (Fig. 1-7)

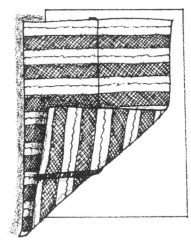

Fig. 1-7: Even feeding.

✂ Speedy volume production—The serger's quick seaming and finishing make light work of traditionally difficult-to-sew projects, such as curtains and multiple costumes. (Fig. 1-8)

Fig. 1-5: Pucker-free sewing.

> *People who don't own a serger think all they're good for is to sew knits. Wrong!*
>
> *Sue Green-Baker*

Fig. 1-8: Speedy volume production.

Fig. 1-9: **Decorative accents.**

✃ **Decorative accents**—Although the sewing machine offers many decorative possibilities, the serger provides still more alternatives, many of which are featured in fashionable ready-to-wear. Decorative seaming, edging, and flatlocking are just the beginning of the many ornamental serging options available. (Fig. 1-9)

How to Use This Book

ABCs of Serging is a step-by-step guide to help the first-time serger user master basic serging and avoid any pitfalls or frustrations. For best results, work through the chapters in order without skipping around, practicing each skill as you proceed.

> *Keep a notebook or workbook near your serger to save the best portion of all your test samples. Also record machine settings and other pertinent notes. Later, you can easily refer to them to refresh your memory and help plan future projects. If you teach, the samples will be invaluable as visuals.*
> *Naomi Baker*

After you've had more serging experience and know some of the basics, keep this book handy. Review those techniques you use less often by looking them up in the table of contents or the index. Or glance through the book occasionally to recall handy techniques and applications you may have forgotten.

> *For quick reference, I keep a chart of tension settings with samples attached on the bulletin board in my sewing area.*
> *Jan Saunders*

Read the boxed pointers from our National Serger Teachers Advisory Board included throughout the text. The board members, profiled at the beginning of this book, are well-known serging professionals with extensive hands-on teaching experience. We asked each of them to give you tips and hints as you learn, just as if you were sitting in on one of their classes or seminars.

When you come to a term you don't understand or have forgotten from an earlier chapter, refer to our Glossary of Serging Terms at the end of the book. For example, when we refer to a straight-stitch, we mean straight-stitching on a conventional sewing machine, using a single line of stitching. You'll find a definition in the glossary.

If you are not able to find locally some of the thread and notions we mention in the text, you can purchase them through the mail. See Reliable Mail-order Sources, which follows the glossary, for a listing of our favorite serging supply sources.

Serger Shopping Guidelines

Whether you are purchasing your first serger, trading up, or buying a second model (perhaps you want to leave one permanently adjusted for rolled edges?), you should follow a few simple guidelines.

1. Shop serger dealers **in your area** and ask about service and education. Both are very important factors for the long-term enjoyment of your machine. Many brands are comparable—the dealer makes the difference.

2. Decide what you will use the serger for. Finishing seams? Decorative techniques? Dressmaking? Draperies? All-purpose serging? Some brands and models are better suited for certain functions (rolled edges, decorative serging, heavy fabrics) than others. Skim through this book to learn more about the options available to you. When you make a purchasing decision, keep in mind that no one serger does everything best. And, as a general rule, the more stitch types a machine offers, the more complicated it will be to use. *For the best value, purchase a serger not for what you may need someday, but for what you will use often now.*

3. Have the dealer show you the various features of each serger and recommend the best ones for your serging needs. Ask about the standard and optional features (see Chapter 2) that interest you.

4. Test any machines that meet the previous guidelines. Take along swatches of the fabric types you'll be using most. If you're interested in decorative serging, also bring some pearl cotton and rayon thread. If necessary, ask the dealer for help with threading and adjusting. Spend some time using the machines, and see how you like the results.

> *Don't let a salesperson do all the testing for you. Consider taking a small group class to learn about sergers and get some hands-on experience before making your final purchasing decision.*
> **Sue Green-Baker**

5. Check to see if an instructional workbook is available for your model. Some manufacturers also offer brand- or model-specific videos to help you learn more quickly.

> *Read the manual and try to follow the instructions to perform a special function on that model. Be sure the directions are clear and easy to understand.*
> **Gale Grigg Hazen**

We are often asked which serger brand and model we recommend, but that's impossible to answer accurately. There are no "bad" machines on the market and there are no "perfect" ones either. Each has its unique advantages. The key to your serging pleasure is finding the one that is best for your specific needs.

2

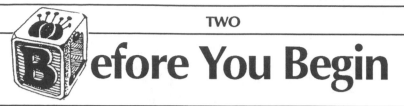

TWO

Before You Begin

✂ Basic Serger Features
✂ Optional Serger Features
✂ Handy Serging Supplies

Before you begin, you'll probably need to purchase a serger and serging supplies. Prior to shopping, review the guidelines suggested in Chapter 1. Then keep the information in this chapter handy when making your purchasing decisions. If you already own a serger, check to see which of the features described in this chapter is available on your model.

Basic Serger Features

Stitch types

A few serger models have only one stitch available, but most sergers feature a combination of stitches. You'll select which stitch to use based on the task at hand and the desired result. Before purchasing your machine, consider your serging needs. Then calculate which stitches will be most useful to you.

2-thread overedge stitch (Fig. 2-1)—Available on some sergers, this stitch uses one needle thread and one looper thread. The looper thread lies on top of the fabric while the needle thread is pulled to the edge on the underside. Because the two threads don't form a locking stitch at the needleline, it is called an "overedge" rather than an "overlock" stitch. Uses include:

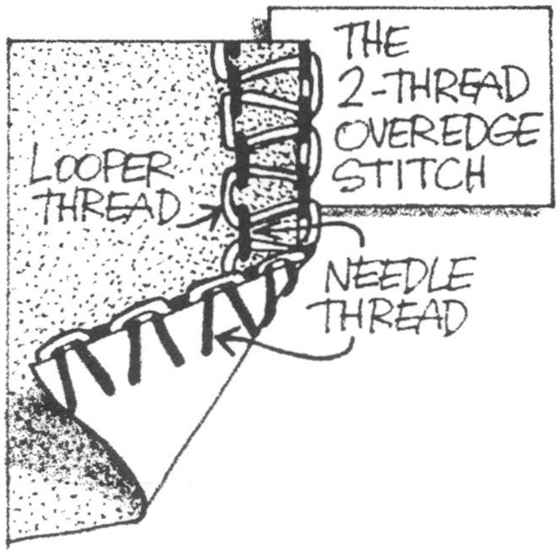

Fig. 2-1: **Formed with a needle thread and a looper thread.**

✂ *Edge-finishing*—less bulky than a 3-thread stitch, preferable for finishing lightweight or delicate fabrics.

✂ *Flatlocking*—ideal for lightweight flatlocked seaming and decorative flatlocking without any adjustment. (You'll learn all about flatlocking in Chapter 13.)

✂ *Rolled edging*—some models also have a 2-thread rolled-edge capability, which is useful for lightweight fabrics.

> ***You can also loosen the lower looper and tighten the needle tension to form a 2-thread reversible stitch. The lower looper thread will show on both sides, while the needle thread won't show and only holds the decorative lower looper thread in place.***
>
> ***Ronda Chaney***

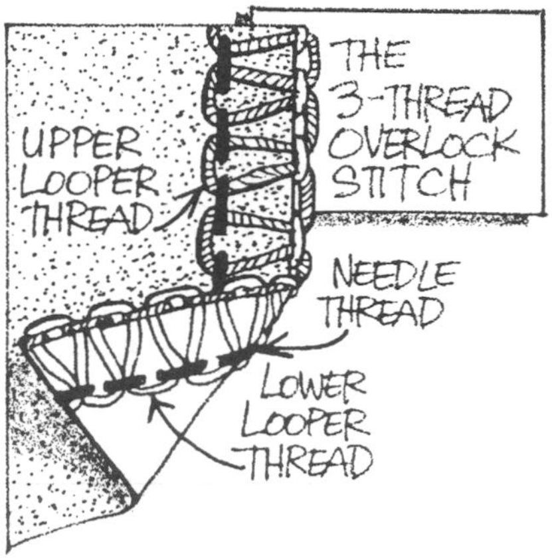

Fig. 2-2: **Formed with a needle thread and two looper threads.**

3-thread overlock stitch (Fig. 2-2)—The most common serger stitch, found on practically every serger model, a 3-thread overlock has one needle thread combined with an upper-looper and lower-looper thread. The upper-looper thread lies on top of the fabric and the lower-looper thread lies on the underside. The looper threads interlock with each other at the edge of the fabric and with the needle thread at the seamline. Uses include:

✂ *Seaming*—makes a very stretchy seam, ideal for knits. It is also suitable for wovens, but may need additional reinforcement for areas of stress.

✂ *Edge-finishing*—good seam finish. Also excellent for balanced-tension, decorative stitching using specialty threads.

✂ *Flatlocking (with tension adjustments)*—used for flatlocked seaming and decorative flatlocking.

✁ *Rolled edging (with adjustments)*—available on most machines. A little heavier than a 2-thread rolled edge, and the most common type.

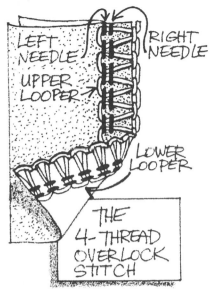

Fig. 2-3: **Formed with two needle threads and two looper threads.**

4-thread overlock stitch (3/4-thread stitch) (Fig. 2-3)—Popular for durable seaming, this wide stitch is formed just like the 3-thread overlock, except a second needle thread is added for security. The looper threads interlock with both needles, so you can convert to a 3-thread overlock stitch by removing either needle. When you are using the left needle only, the stitch will be wider than when you are using the right needle only. Some 4-thread machines can also convert to a 2-thread overedge stitch. Uses include:

✁ *Seaming*—more durable than a 3-thread stitch, but not quite as stretchy. This stitch is ideal for stress areas on garments, such as active wear or children's wear, and for ravelly fabric. It can be used on knits as well as wovens because it stretches.

✁ *Edge-finishing*—durable decorative finishing for edges or seams, but bulkier than a 2- or 3-thread finish.

✁ *Flatlocking (with tension adjustments)*—can be converted to a flatlock.

✁ *Rolled edging*—must be converted to a 3-thread stitch before adjusting for this stitch.

> **The 4-thread overlock stitch has the advantage of a safety stitch. If the seamline thread breaks, the second row of stitching prevents the seam allowance from ravelling out.**
> **Jan Saunders**

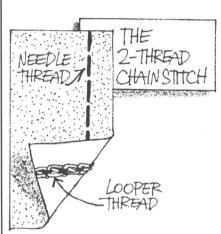

Fig. 2-4: **Formed with a needle thread and a looper thread, but does not overcast the edge.**

2-thread chainstitch (Fig. 2-4)—A needle thread and a looper thread create this stitch, which looks much like a conventional straight-stitch on the top side of the fabric. The needle thread passes through the fabric, interlocking with the looper thread, creating a chain-like stitch on the reverse side. It is stable with little to no stretch. This stitch type is offered on sergers only in combination with other serged stitches. Uses include:

✁ *Seaming*—usually combined with the 2-thread overedge or the 3-thread overlock stitch, but can be used by itself to serge a seam.

✁ *Decorative detailing*—unlike other serger stitches that must be sewn on an edge or fold, the chainstitch can be placed a distance away. With decorative thread, it can be used for topstitching or other detailing.

> **The 2-thread chainstitch is also a good basting stitch, because it will unravel easily for removal.**
> **Naomi Baker**

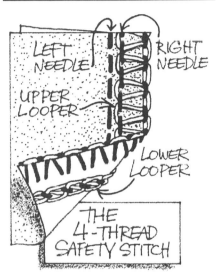

Fig. 2-5: **Formed with a chainstitch and a 2-thread overedge stitch.**

4-thread safety stitch (4/2-thread stitch) (Fig. 2-5)—This wide stitch combines the 2-thread overedge stitch and the 2-thread chainstitch, using two needles and two loopers. Usually both the 2-thread chain and the 2-thread overedge stitch can be used independently, and the model will feature other stitch types as well. Uses include:

✁ *Seaming*—stable on loosely woven, ravelly fabric. Because the chainstitch portion of the stitch has little or no stretch, the 4-thread safety stitch is not recommended for stretchable knit seaming.

✁ *Edge-finishing*—stable finish, especially on ravelly fabric. Not often used for decorative edging.

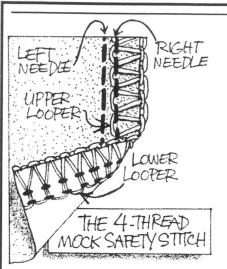

Fig. 2-6: Formed with two needle threads and two looper threads, but not available on the same machine as a 4-thread overlock stitch.

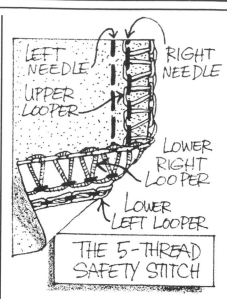

Fig. 2-7: Formed with a chainstitch and a 3-thread overlock stitch.

4-thread mock safety stitch (Fig. 2-6)—Available on a few models, this wide stitch uses two loopers and two needles. It is similar to the 4-thread overlock stitch except, from the topside, it looks like the 5-thread safety stitch—the upper-looper thread interlocks with the right needle thread only and does not extend to the left needle. On the underside, the lower looper interlocks with both needles and extends the full width of the stitch, just the same as on the 4-thread overlock.

Note: When converting a 4-thread mock safety stitch to a 3-thread overlock stitch, *only the right needle can be used,* forming a narrow stitch. Models with the 4-thread mock safety stitch do not have the capability of a wide, 3-thread stitch. Uses include:

✂ *Seaming*—more durable than a 3-thread stitch, but not as stretchy. It is ideal for stress areas on active wear or children's wear and for ravelly fabric. It can be used on knits as well as wovens because it does stretch some.

✂ *Edge-finishing*—stable finish, especially on ravelly fabric. Not often used for decorative edging.

5-thread safety stitch (Fig. 2-7)—This extra-wide (approximately 7mm to 8mm) stitch is formed by a 2-thread chainstitch and a 3-thread overlock stitch. It is created with two needles and three loopers. The left needle and the lower left looper (chainstitch looper) form the chainstitch, while a right needle and the upper and lower right loopers form the overlock stitch. With adjustments, a 5-thread machine can serge the 3-thread overlock stitch or the chainstitch independently, and one or more of the other stitch options are also available. Uses include:

✂ *Seaming*—similar to the 4-thread safety stitch, the 5-thread stitch is very stable and recommended for loosely woven and ravelly fabrics or for stress-prone seams and edges. Because the chainstitch cannot stretch, the stitch should be used for stable knits or wovens only.

✂ *Edge-finishing*—the most stable finish, but not often used for decorative purposes.

Tension adjustments

Tension controls (all containing tension discs) are used to vary the appearance or function of a stitch by controlling the speed at which the thread is fed through the loopers and needles. If the controls are round knobs on the front of the machine, the thread wraps around the knobs, sliding between two tension discs. If the controls are inset dials, the thread is laid vertically into slot-like openings at the top of the machine and engaged between the discs. (Fig. 2-8)

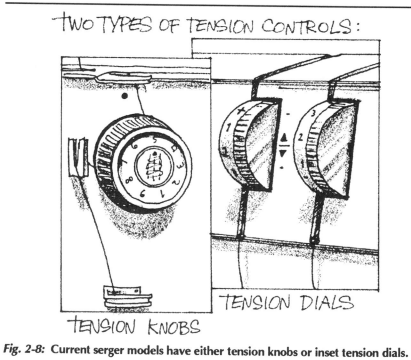

Fig. 2-8: Current serger models have either tension knobs or inset tension dials.

The uptake on a sewing machine is responsible for pulling enough thread from the spool for the next stitch. A serger does not have an uptake. Its method for allotting the correct portion of thread for each stitch is adjustment of the tension mechanism. For a shorter or narrower stitch, the tension mechanism is adjusted to squeeze tighter on the thread, allowing less thread for the stitch. Very long or wide overlock stitches need more thread, so the mechanism is loosened.
Gale Grigg Hazen

Some sergers have numbered controls for easier tension setting, while others simply have plus (+) and minus (-) symbols to indicate the direction for tightening or loosening. Many machines also have helpful labels or symbols to indicate which knob or dial controls which looper or needle. Some of the latest models are designed with tension controls located closer to the corresponding looper or needle for more accurate tension adjustment.

If your tension controls aren't labeled and you tend to forget which control is for which thread, write the names on small pieces of masking tape. Place each label near or on the correct control (identify them in your owner's manual to be sure). Leave the controls labeled until you know them by heart.
Ruthann Spiegelhoff

Changing the tension settings is not complicated if you follow a few basic guidelines. You'll learn all the details in Chapter 6.

Stitch length adjustment

Stitch length is adjusted with a dial or lever. The higher the number, the longer the stitch, and, conversely, the lower the number, the shorter the stitch. On many sergers the stitch length control is conveniently located on the outside of the machine so you can adjust it while serging. Chapter 7 will lead you through stitch length adjustment.

The stitch adjustment on a serger is similar to a conventional sewing machine. The length of the needle's straight-stitch (north and south) is the stitch length. The width controls the zigzag (east-west) part of the stitch.
Sue Green-Baker

Stitch width adjustment

Methods for changing the stitch width vary widely. (Fig. 2-9) On some sergers, the width is fully adjustable within a preset range. On others, you'll have only a few width options. The most convenient stitch width control is a dial or lever that changes the width by moving the knife to cut away more or less fabric from the seam allowance. On other machines, you adjust the width by manually moving the knife or changing the stitch finger for a wider or narrower stitch. On 4-thread overlock models (see page 9), removing the left needle will narrow the stitch width.

When shopping for a serger, evaluate the range of stitch widths available, the ease in changing the width, and whether the width control is conveniently located. Chapter 7 will help you practice stitch width adjustment, no matter what type of controls your serger has.

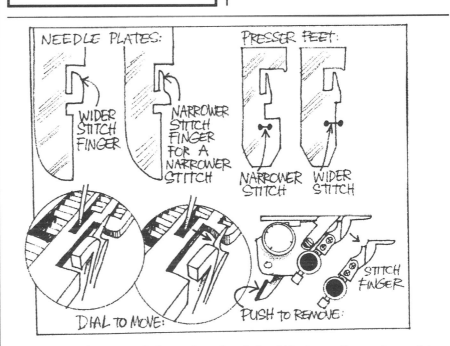

Fig. 2-9: Changing the stitch finger alters the stitch width. Depending on the model, the stitch finger can be part of a needle plate or a presser foot. Or it can be a separate part, easily moved or removed by a dial or lever.

Rolled-edge adjustment

Some machines have a built-in rolled-edge setting—a lever or dial is used to change or alter the stitch finger. On other machines, you'll need to change the needle plate, the presser foot, or both. All serger models require stitch width, stitch length, and tension adjustments to convert to a rolled-edge stitch from balanced serging. You'll practice rolled edges in Chapter 14.

Other features

Check for other features that are often standard, such as a built-in light, a waste container, a built-in thread cutter, and convenient accessory storage. Additional basic features to be considered when purchasing a serger or when getting to know your own serger are: maximum stitch width capacity, maximum stitching speed, stitch length capacity, accessories included, and overall ease of use.

Optional Serger Features

Most serger models on the market today have additional features that come on or with the machine or are available for purchase.

Fig. 2-10: Some standard presser feet have built-in guides to position cording or tape while it is being serged over.

Specialty feet

Some machines have special features built into the standard presser foot:

✄ **Snap-on feet** can be easily switched or removed for threading or needle changing. (Fig. 2-10)

✄ **Elastic/tape guide** or a **cording guide** for ease and accuracy in serging over thread, cording, tape, elastic, or other filler. This feature is especially handy for decorative serging applications and for certain utility tasks, such as stabilizing a seam or gathering.

Optional presser feet are also made for most serger models. (Fig. 2-11) Some of the following may be available for your machine; check with your dealer for information:

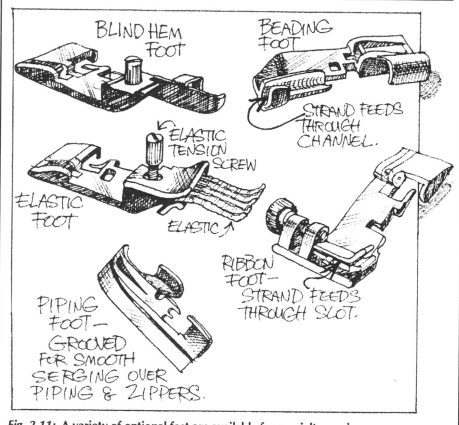

Fig. 2-11: A variety of optional feet are available for specialty serging.

- ✂ blindhem foot
- ✂ beading/pearl/sequin foot
- ✂ elastic/tape foot
- ✂ ribbon/tape foot
- ✂ piping/cording foot

Threading features

To alleviate the sometimes difficult and time-consuming task of threading a serger, many manufacturers have built in easy-threading features. These include self-threading lower loopers, built-in needle threaders, easily accessible thread guides, a swing-out presser foot, and color-coded threading systems.

Differential feed

A very useful option available on many serger models is the differential feed. An adjustment knob or lever varies the speed of the machine's two sets of feed dogs, controlling how taut or compacted the fabric is while being serged over. Differential feeding can prevent stretching of knits and puckering of fine or sheer fabrics. It can also be used for gathering or easing. In Chapter 8 you'll learn how to use the differential feed.

Presser-foot pressure regulator

Especially on sergers without differential feed, regulating the presser-foot pressure can help prevent stretching, puckering, and skipped stitches. You'll learn more about this control feature in Chapter 8.

Disengaging knife

All sergers have two knives that work together to trim the fabric edge while serging. Sometimes, however, you won't want to trim the edge (for example, when serging elastic, serging over a fold, or top-stitching with the 2-thread chainstitch). In this case, you'll appreciate the optional feature (available on some machines) of disengaging one of the knives so there is no chance of inadvertently cutting the edge. (Fig. 2-12)

Although disengaging the knife is a helpful feature, as a repair person, I want to caution you about the potential dangers of serging while it is disengaged. The reason all sergers have cutting blades is to make sure the edge of the fabric does not stick out past the right edge of the needle plate. If it does, it will be in the way of the upper looper path. The high speed of the loopers will cause a violent impact when they slam into the fabric. This is one of the leading causes of extensive serger repair. Sew very slowly and carefully when the knife is disengaged, and guide the fabric accurately.

Gale Grigg Hazen

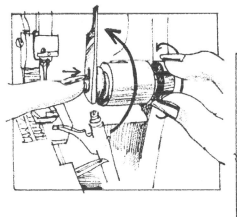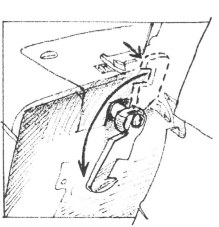

Fig. 2-12: On some machines you can disengage the knife.

Computerized stitch guide

Some newer serger models have a computerized liquid crystal display (LCD). After you enter the desired stitch, the panel indicates the necessary tension, stitch length, and differential feed settings, as well as the position of the needles, knives, and loopers.

Safety features

To prevent injury, all home serger models have some type of knife guard. Some machines also have guards to keep fingers away from the moving needles and exposed upper looper. On some sergers the power automatically shuts off when the front and side covers are opened.

Other features

Additional features (available on only some serger models) include:

✄ Bias binder—used with a 2-thread chainstitch to fold, position, and attach a bias binding strip.

✄ Fabric separator—used with differential feed to gather one layer of fabric as it is serge-seamed to a nongathered layer.

✄ Tape or cording guides—used to position tape or cording before it reaches the presser foot and is serged over.

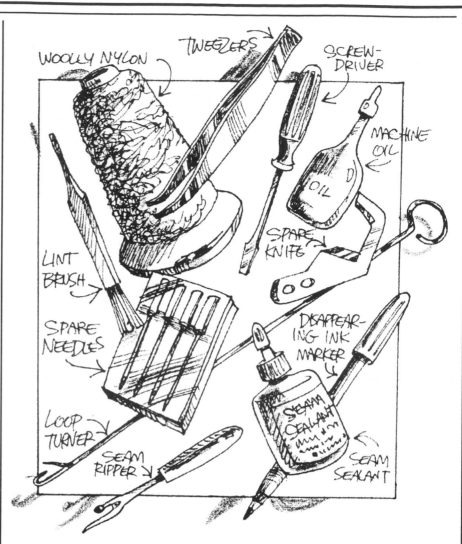

Fig. 2-13: Keep your serging supplies close at hand.

✄ Stitching guides (also called cloth guides, edge guides, or ornamental serging guides)—used to position the fabric accurately as it is fed through the machine.

✄ Special needle plate—used for extra-wide stitches.

✄ Free-arm—used for finishing hard-to-reach areas.

Handy Serging Supplies

Before you begin serging, collect the necessary equipment and supplies: (Fig. 2-13)

✄ Serger

✄ Owner's manual

✄ Brand- or model-specific workbook and/or video (if available)

- ✂ Note cards or notebook to record test results and samples
- ✂ Accessories and attachments included with the machine
- ✂ Serger (or all-purpose) thread—three to five cones or spools (one for each thread path on your machine)

As you're learning to serge, select a different thread color for each spool or cone. When you're adjusting the tensions and perfecting the stitches, you can identify each thread much more easily. If your machine has colored symbols defining the various thread paths, match the thread color to the symbols.
Sue Green-Baker

- ✂ Specialty thread (such as woolly nylon, monofilament nylon, fusible thread, pearl cotton, and other decorative threads)
- ✂ Needle-nose pliers or a needle inserter
- ✂ Spare machine needles
- ✂ Spare machine knife (one usually comes with the serger)
- ✂ Seam sealant
- ✂ Transparent tape
- ✂ A loop turner, knit picker, latch hook, or darning needle to secure seam ends
- ✂ Disappearing marking pens (both washable and air-erasable)
- ✂ Clear elastic (most helpful in 3/8" and 1/2" widths)
- ✂ Elastic thread or cording
- ✂ Water-soluble stabilizer
- ✂ Other conventional sewing supplies
- ✂ A conventional sewing machine
- ✂ Fabric swatches for testing

As you proceed through this book, it is important to test each stitch and technique. Stable, mediumweight fabrics are the easiest to test-serge, but as you progress, you'll want to test other fabric types as well—knits, lightweights, heavier weights, and various textures. Cut long strips, approximately 4" wide. Longer strips are beneficial for practicing and perfecting the stitch, because you can test a few inches, look at the stitching behind the foot, make any necessary adjustments, and continue perfecting the stitch without having to serge on and off short swatches of fabric.
Gail Brown

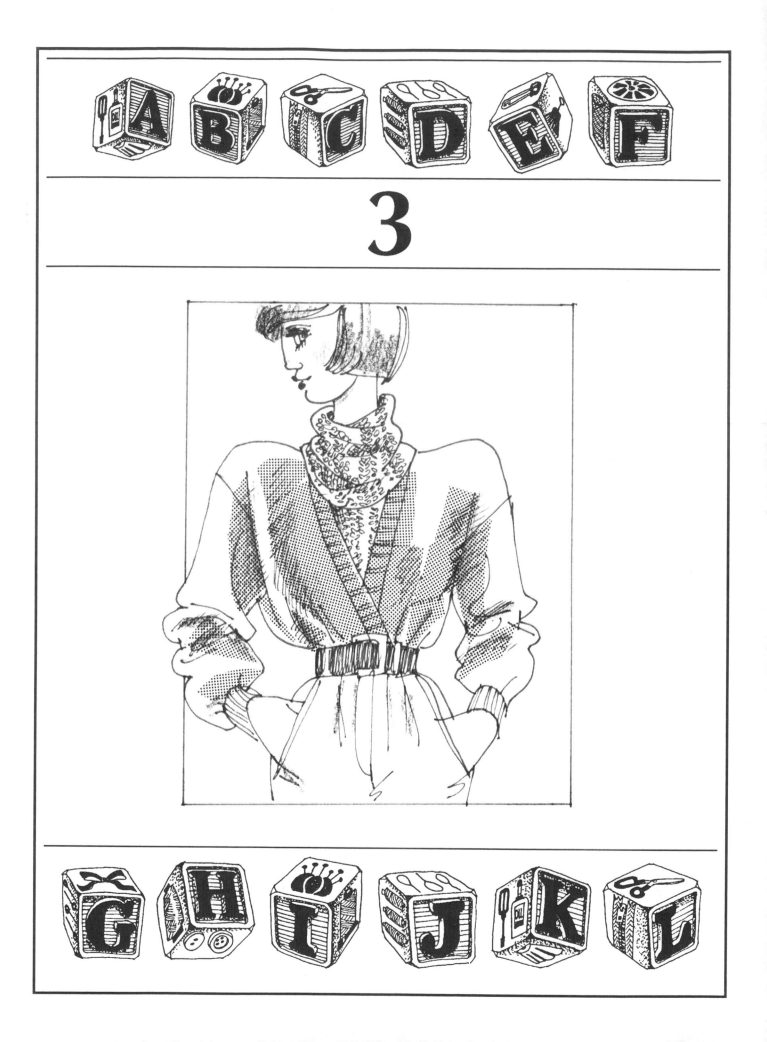

3

Check Out Your Equipment

✂ Set Up the Machine
✂ Identify and Define the Parts
✂ Know Your Accessories

Before you begin serging with any model, take time to familiarize yourself with the parts of that machine and the accessories available. Think of it as if you're checking out all the operating features on a car you've never driven. It won't take long, and you'll feel much more comfortable when you begin to use it.

Set Up the Machine

Reorganize your sewing area

The first step, even before taking your serger out of the box, is to find a place to put it. Because the serger works in tandem with your sewing machine, you'll need to move easily from one machine to the other for maximum productivity.

Reorganize your sewing space so that you can reach both machines comfortably. There should be adequate room between the serger and sewing machine for natural work flow (we recommend 24"). A rolling chair (on a plastic mat over carpeting) makes maneuvering between the machines

Fig. 3-1: Position both the sewing machine and serger so they can be used comfortably.

much easier. Find a sturdy, flat surface which will position the machine beds approximately 28" from the floor for minimum neck and back strain. (Fig. 3-1) Ideally, you'll want to keep the serger set up without having to put it away every time you sew. Some of us cannot afford this luxury, however, and must find creative ways of storing our machines so they are easily and quickly accessible.

> *Robbie Fanning stores her serger on a rolling computer stand in a closet so she can roll it out to a convenient position for use.*
> *Jan Saunders*

Set up the machine

Take the serger out of the box. This may seem a formidable, frightening experience for some. Don't procrastinate: just lift the machine out of the packing material and place it on the table or stand you've selected. Remove the owner's manual and all other parts and accessories. Save the box and packing material in case you ever need to transport the machine.

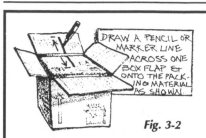

DRAW A PENCIL OR MARKER LINE ACROSS ONE BOX FLAP & ONTO THE PACKING MATERIAL AS SHOWN.

Fig. 3-2

Before removing anything from the box, open the top and draw a line across one box flap, continuing the mark onto the foam packing material. (Fig. 3-2) (There is no need to mark the bottom section of foam if you're leaving it in the box.) Then, when repacking the machine, just line up the markings. If you don't do this, putting the machine away can seem like a jigsaw puzzle.
Sue Green-Baker

Position the front of the serger approximately 4" from the table edge. Because it was probably oiled thoroughly at the factory, wipe off any parts that may touch the fabric. Use a soft, clean, lint-free cloth. If your spool base (the support on which the spools or cones sit during serging) isn't assembled, attach it now, following instructions provided (usually in the owner's manual).

Read the owner's manual from cover to cover. It may be difficult to understand (some manuals are not clearly written), but try to plow through it as best you can. At the very least, you'll learn the type of information included so you can refer to it later.
Gale Grigg Hazen

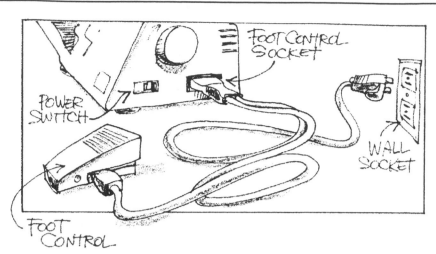

FOOT CONTROL SOCKET
POWER SWITCH
WALL SOCKET
FOOT CONTROL

Fig. 3-3: Plug the foot control into the machine socket, then into the household socket.

Read your owner's manual through while sitting in front of your serger. It's less boring, and the instructions and drawings will make much more sense.
Jan Saunders

Hook up the foot control

The foot control is attached to a cord with a machine plug and a standard household electrical plug, similar to the control on most conventional sewing machines. Plug the foot control into the machine socket first, then the household socket. The machine socket is usually located on the lower right side of the machine. If you can't find it, refer to the machine diagram in your owner's manual. (Fig. 3-3)

Now you're ready to turn on the power. On many sergers the power switch controls both the power and the light. If you leave the machine, be sure to turn off the power. The power switch is usually located near the machine socket (check your owner's manual).

Identify and Define the Parts

Open your owner's manual to the machine diagram. Double-check to see that the model number in the diagram is the same as your machine. Read about the machine parts listed below and locate them on your serger. (They are listed here in alphabetical order for easy reference.) Due to brand and model variations, our generic diagrams may not match your machine exactly, but will provide a general concept of the appearance.

Photocopy the owner's-manual illustration of your model, and make notes on it as you read this chapter.
Naomi Baker

Differential feed selector (not available on all models)— a knob or lever located on the side of the serger by the handwheel or under a side or front cover by the stitch length lever. (Refer back to page 13 for a brief description of differential feed. You'll learn how to use it in Chapter 8.)

Feed dogs—rows of metal teeth located under the presser foot. The feed dogs work similarly to those on a conventional machine, gripping the fabric and pulling it through the machine. (Differential feed works with two separate sets of feed dogs; a front set feeds the fabric in at a different speed than the back set pulls it out.)

Foot control—a pedal that regulates the stitching speed. (See Fig. 3-3) To operate it, press (or let up on) the control with your foot. Some sergers have an electronic foot control which allows a maximum speed change with only a small movement of the pedal.

Foot control socket (machine socket)—the opening where the foot-control cord plugs into the machine. (See Fig. 3-3)

Front cover (looper cover)—a protective cover on the front of the machine, keeping lint, fabric, and fingers away from the moving parts. To open the cover, either pull it forward, slide it to the right and then tilt it forward, or release a lever and swing it open to the right. Does your model have a built-in safety system, turning off the power (but not the light) when the cover is open? (Fig. 3-4)

Handwheel (flywheel)—similar to the one on a conventional sewing machine. The handwheel on a serger is usually located on the right side of the machine. It may turn forward (counterclockwise) as on a sewing machine or in the opposite direction (clockwise). It is usually marked with an arrow showing the correct direction. If not, refer to your owner's manual. Be sure to turn the handwheel in the correct direction to prevent broken or tangled threads. (Fig. 3-4)

Serger handwheels should be turned in only one direction. When moved in reverse, the thread chain will become tangled and break. If your serger's handwheel turns in the opposite direction from the one on your sewing machine, tape an arrow on it or tape a large arrow onto the table directly under it to remind yourself until it becomes a habit.
Gale Grigg Hazen

If you forget which direction to turn the handwheel, place your hand on it and touch the foot pedal lightly. You'll feel it start and can continue to turn it in that direction.
Ruthann Spiegelhoff

Knives (cutters)—located in front of the needle(s) on all serger models. Two knives work together like shears to trim the fabric before it is serged. One knife remains stationary (usually the inner, lower knife) while the other moves up

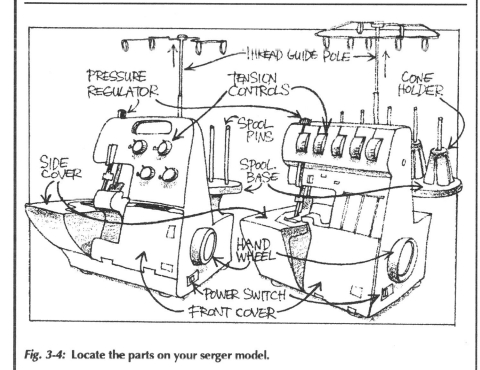

Fig. 3-4: Locate the parts on your serger model.

and down with each stitch of the machine (usually the outer, upper knife). (Fig. 3-5) One knife is made

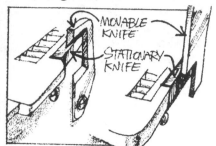

Fig. 3-5: **One stationary and one movable knife work together to cut or trim.**

of a strong carbide steel that doesn't wear as quickly as the other, softer blade. If a pin is accidentally hit, the softer, less expensive blade gives and is damaged, while the harder blade will resist and usually will not need replacing.

Check for blade sharpness by serging a scrap of nylon tricot. Dull cutting edges won't cut tricot at all.
Sue Green-Baker

If the cut edge of the fabric is ragged, check the knives. Replace knives with worn or nicked blades. Also check for an improperly positioned knife. (The lower, inner knife blade should be even with the top of the needle plate.) See your owner's manual for information on how to change and position the knife.

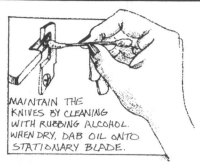

Fig. 3-6

You can prolong the life of a serger knife by simple cleaning and lubricating. Lint can build up between the knives, causing them to spread slightly. Move the blades away from each other to clean between them. (If you don't have a knife that disengages, you may need to loosen a screw to separate the blades.) Clean the knife surfaces regularly with rubbing alcohol on a cotton swab. When dry, apply a small amount of oil to the stationary blade. (Fig. 3-6) Serge a scrap to be sure any excess oil is wiped off and won't ruin your good fabric.
Gale Grigg Hazen

If you do loosen a screw to separate the blades, they need to be accurately realigned before serging again. Check your owner's manual or have your dealer show you if you are unsure how to do this.
Sue Green-Baker

✄ **Loopers**—shaped metal fingers used to position thread when forming a serged stitch. The loopers available on your machine depend on the stitch types your

machine was designed to perform (stitch types are described in Chapter 1). A thread passes through a hole (called an eye) at the end of each looper being used. To form a basic 3-thread stitch, the upper looper goes over the top of the fabric, leaving a thread loop that is caught by the needle thread on the seamline. At the same time, the lower looper goes under the fabric to catch the needle thread. At the edge of the fabric, the looper threads interlock with each other. (Fig. 3-7)

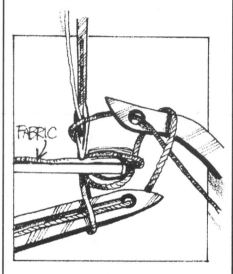

Fig. 3-7: **The upper and lower loopers work with the needle to form a 3-thread stitch. The timing is essential.**

✄ **Needle(s)**—either one or two are necessary for every serger stitch. Needle requirements vary from one serger model to another.

To avoid problems, don't interchange different brands of needles.
Sue Green-Baker

Consult your owner's manual or dealer to verify which needle size and type your machine uses. Three general categories of needles are available—household, industrial, and custom:

Household needles are the same type as those used on conventional sewing machines. One side of the shank is flat, making them easy to insert.

Industrial needles are more durable to withstand the stress of fast serger stitching. They vary in the length of the needle and the position of the eye and often have a round shank. Insert industrial needles with the scarf (the short indentation that extends from just below the needle eye to partway up the shaft) toward the back and the long groove toward the front. (Fig. 3-8)

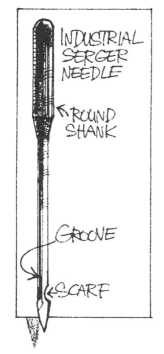

Fig. 3-8: Industrial needles usually have a round shank. Position the scarf to the back and the groove to the front.

> **Find the long groove by running your thumbnail down the length of the needle.**
> **Jan Saunders**

Custom needles are those that have been specially designed to fit a particular serger model.

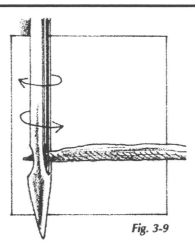

Fig. 3-9

> **Round-shank, industrial or custom needles may be difficult to insert with the eye facing straight from front to back. For correct alignment, place the needle in the shaft, place a toothpick in the eye, and adjust the needle until the toothpick is facing forward. (Fig. 3-9)**
> **Gale Grigg Hazen**

✂ **Needle plate**—a flat metal plate, located on the bed of the machine, under the presser foot and around the feed dogs. (Fig. 3-10) Some models have only one needle plate, while others have specialized ones for rolled edges or wider stitching.

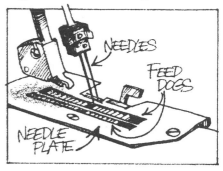

Fig. 3-10: The needle plate is located on the machine bed. On some models, additional needle plates are supplied for rolled edges and/or wider stitching.

✂ **Power switch**—controls all the power to the serger, usually located on the lower right side of the machine. (See Fig. 3-3) Some models may have separate power and light switches or a single power switch with a separate setting, enabling the light to be on with the rest of the machine's power off.

✂ **Presser-foot pressure regulator (not available on all models)**—adjusts the amount of force applied to the fabric by the presser foot. Available on most models, it is a screw on the top of the machine similar to those on many sewing machines. When you purchase your machine, the factory has preset the pressure. It seldom needs adjusting for basic serging, even when you are sewing with different weights and textures of fabric. You'll learn more about presser-foot pressure in Chapter 8. (See Fig. 3-4)

> *If your pressure regulator is not marked or numbered, mark it now so you know where "normal" is when you need to adjust it in the future.*
> *Jan Saunders*
>
> *Soft, squishy fabrics become permanently ruffled when stretched out of shape by too much pressure. On a serger without a differential feed, learn to use the presser-foot regulator so you can fine-tune your technique.*
> *Gale Grigg Hazen*

✄ **Presser foot**—holds the fabric against the feed dogs as the serger stitches. Check to see if your model's standard presser foot has built-in features such as a cording guide or an elastic/tape guide. Are optional presser feet (listed on pages 12 - 13) available for your machine? Does your serger have a swing-out foot for easier access to the needle or snap-on presser feet for quick changes as well as better access?

✄ **Presser-foot lever**—raises the presser foot. Usually located at the rear of the machine above the presser foot (or sometimes on the right side). Lift the lever until it engages. On some models, the lever can be lifted an additional distance to provide maximum space between the presser foot and the needle plate.

✄ **Side cover (cloth plate)**—to keep lint and fabric away from the moving parts. (See Fig. 3-4) Most side covers swing open to the left. Some have a release lever that must be pressed before or during opening. As with the front cover, your serger may have an automatic power shutoff when the side cover is opened.

✄ **Spool base**—the support on which thread spools sit during serging. It is usually located on the back of the machine and spool pins are attached to the base. Some models are not boxed with the spool base assembled, so you must put it on yourself. If you haven't already, check your owner's manual to see how it's attached. (See Fig. 3-4)

> *Some spool bases slide to the right to allow more room for the fabric to move through the machine. Check to see if your model has this feature. It's handy, because your project won't hang up on the spool base.*
> *Jan Saunders*

✄ **Stitch finger**—a metal prong located behind the knives (sometimes as part of the needle plate or the presser foot, or as a separate piece). The threads loop around the stitch finger while forming the stitch. (Fig. 3-11) Some models

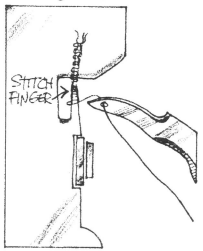

Fig. 3-11: **The thread loops around the stitch finger to form the stitch.**

have stitch fingers in several sizes so you can vary the stitch width. This may mean changing the needle plate or presser foot to change the stitch width. For easier stitch width adjustment, some models have a lever or dial to expedite a stitch finger change or a width change on the same stitch finger. (Chapter 7 gives you step-by-step details.)

✂ **Stitch length selector**—often a dial or lever used to adjust the stitch length. On other models, you'll press a release button while turning the handwheel to change the stitch length setting. The method varies from model to model, so check your owner's manual. Turn to the highest number for the longest stitch and the lowest number for the shortest stitch. We'll discuss stitch length adjustment in Chapter 7.

✂ **Stitch width selector**—varies widely among machines. Some sergers have a stitch width selector that moves the knife position. Others have two needles, and by omitting one needle, you can vary the width. On some machines you change the stitch finger to change the stitch width. (In Chapter 7, you'll practice changing the stitch width on your machine.)

✂ **Tension controls**—either knobs or inset dials (see page 10). Inside each tension control are two discs. The thread runs between them, and the amount of pressure exerted determines how much tension is placed on the thread. Tension controls are used to vary the appearance or function of a stitch. (In Chapter 6, you'll learn how to regulate serger tension controls.)

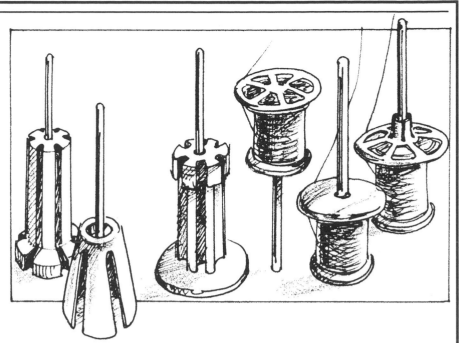

Fig. 3-12: **Spool caps and cone holders will stabilize spools and cones, allowing for even feeding.**

✂ **Thread guides**—slots, holes, or hooks through which the thread passes on its way to a looper or needle. Each thread has several guides. A missed thread guide can result in poor stitch quality.

✂ **Thread-guide pole**—a support rod at the back of the machine that holds the initial thread guides to draw the thread evenly from all the spools and prevent it from tangling. Be sure the thread-guide pole is extended to its highest point or the stitching may be uneven. (See Fig. 3-4)

Know Your Accessories

✂ **Cone holders**—placed onto the spool pins to support cones or large spools of thread. Cone holders vary in shape and size from manufacturer to manufacturer. Some machines come with cone holders preattached to the spool pins. (Fig. 3-12)

✂ **Lint brush**—a stiff-bristled brush used to clean the lint and trimmings from the machine workings. It's important to keep the area around the serger's moving parts as lint-free as possible. (See Serger Care and Maintenance at the end of this book.)

Dab the end of the brush with a little sewing-machine oil to clean the lint from hard-to-reach areas. It catches the lint and leaves a small amount of oil for lubricating.
Jan Saunders

Makeup brushes are softer and fuller than the lint brushes that come with the machine. They quickly and easily remove lots of lint from the serger's working parts.
Ronda Chaney

If tenacious lint won't go away with forced air or soft serger-cleaning brushes, try a small

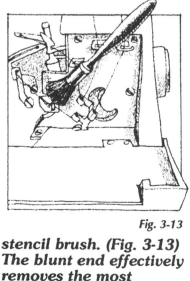

Fig. 3-13

stencil brush. (Fig. 3-13) The blunt end effectively removes the most stubborn lint. Look for stencil brushes at your local craft shops.
Gail Brown

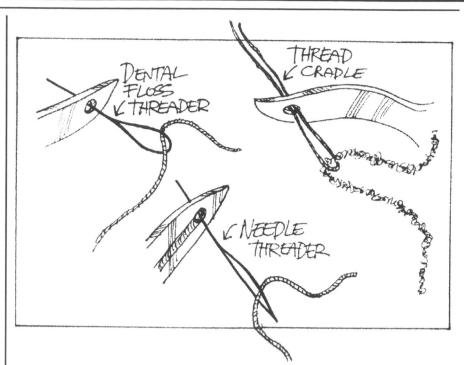

Fig. 3-14: Several types of threaders work well to ease the threading process.

✂ **Looper threader**—helps make threading a looper easier, especially when you are using difficult-to-thread strands, such as woolly nylon or yarn. With the most common type of threader, you'll insert the thread into the large eye. Then push the straight, pointed end of the threader through the looper hole from front to back. Pull the threader with the thread completely through the looper.

A dental-floss threader (available at any drugstore) makes an ideal and inexpensive looper threader. (Fig. 3-14) Place the thread through the plastic loop and feed the single end of the threader through the looper hole. Purchased wire needle or looper threaders and thread cradles also work well.

Because it is so easy to lose dental floss threaders, I tell my students to tape one to the side of their serger.
Ronda Chaney

Looper threaders with short handles also work well. Push the threader through the looper from the back side, put the thread through it, and pull.
Sue Green-Baker

✂ **Oiler**—for proper care and maintenance. It's important to oil your machine regularly—approximately after every fifth garment (except for some newer models that are "self-oiling" and do not require oiling at all). *Use sewing machine oil only;* household oil will be too heavy. Consult your owner's manual for where to oil and how much oil to use.

Screwdrivers—one or two small ones, included with the serger. These are used for changing needles, knives, presser feet, needle plates, or any other parts that may need removing for cleaning, replacing, or switching.

Spare knife—to replace a worn or nicked blade. As explained under Knives, earlier in this chapter on page 20, the softer metal blade will probably need changing first. An extra knife is usually included with the serger. Some sergers are designed for easy knife replacement, but the knife positioning is a precision task—error will affect the cutting quality. Study your manual; if you are uncertain about replacing the knife, let your dealer do it the first time and show you how.

Note: The lower knife (often the softer metal) is usually much easier to replace than the upper knife because the top of the lower blade lines up with the top of the needle plate, allowing for more accurate positioning.

Spool caps—used with conventional, parallel-wound thread spools. They prevent spools from bouncing and thread from getting caught on the spool edge. When using conventional spools on your serger, remove the cone holders, place the spools directly on the pins, and push the caps onto the pins over the spool tops. For machines that have cone holders attached to the spool pins, place the spools onto the pins above the cone holders and place the spool caps directly over the spools. (Fig. 3-12)

Thread nets—net-like tubes that prevent thread from tangling or feeding irregularly. They are particularly useful when you are serging with fine, slippery, or low-twist thread, which is likely to fall loose from the spool. The net tubes go completely over the spool or cone or turn back at the top edge. (Fig. 3-15)

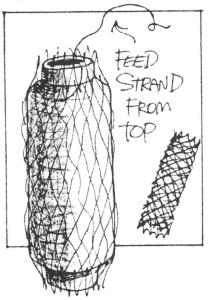

FEED STRAND FROM TOP

Fig. 3-15: Thread nets help the thread feed evenly without tangling.

> *Rayon, monofilament nylon, and some metallic threads will "drool" off the spool. If the thread came with a cellophane wrapper, it may be a hint on how the thread acts when not covered. Make extra nets from recycled pantyhose for known "droolers."*
> **Sue Green-Baker**
>
> *I like having extra nets over the serger cones for storage on a thread rack. The ends won't tangle and my thread stays neat.*
> **Jan Saunders.**

Tweezers—almost essential for threading a serger. Use them for threading loopers, needles, or thread guides or for guiding thread in any limited-space area.

> *I recommend at least one pair of tweezers for the serger and one for the sewing machine for many uses such as:*
> *retrieving a drawstring that has worked its way back into a casing;*
> *pulling out a broken needle from either machine;*
> *holding yarn, cord, or ribbon for couching onto a piece of fabric.*
> **Jan Saunders**

Vinyl machine cover—keeps your serger dust-free when not in use. One is often included with the machine. If not, purchase a cover from a dealer, fabric store, or mail-order serger supply company (see Reliable Mail-order Sources at the end of this book).

> *Don't cover your serger with nonbreathing plastic in humid climates. Instead, cut apart your plastic cover on the heat-pressed seams, and use the sections as a pattern to make a fabric cover.*
> **Sue Green-Baker**

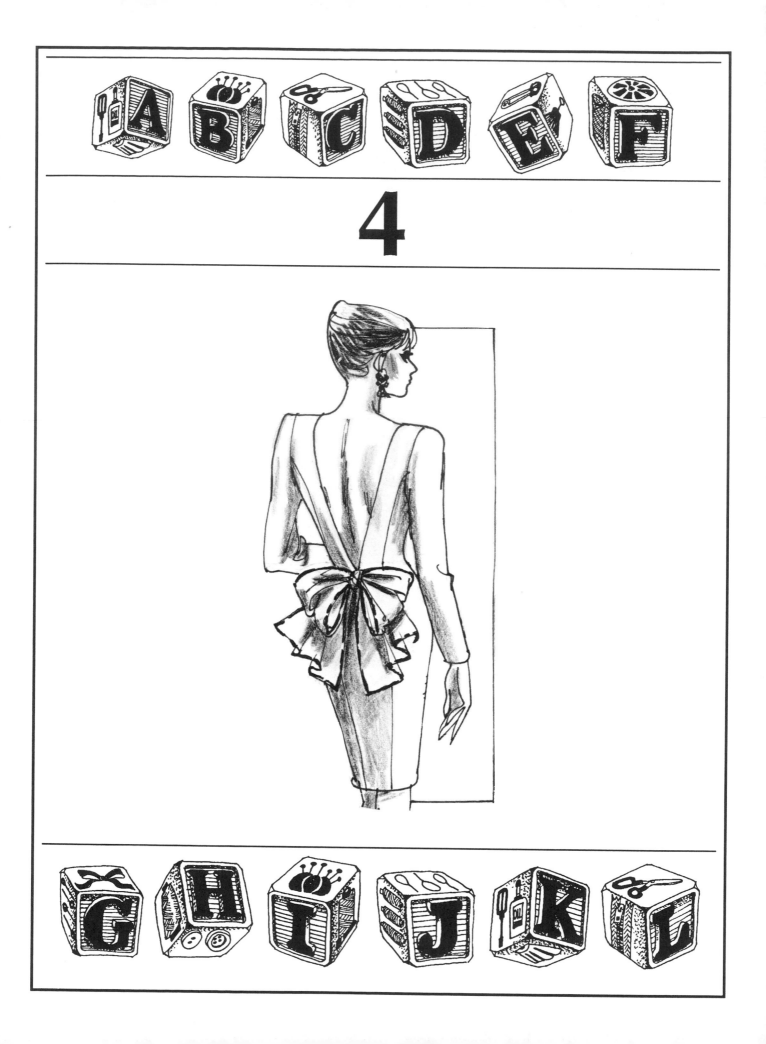

4

Don't Let Threading Intimidate You

✄ **Purchasing Thread**
✄ **Quick-change Threading**
✄ **The Complete Threading Process**
✄ **Threading Troubleshooting**

Threading is **not** something to be afraid of. We'll start right at the beginning, explaining all about different thread types and how to choose quality thread for your serger. Then you'll learn how to change the thread and how to thread your machine from scratch. Take it slowly, reread the text as often as necessary, and **practice.** Threading can be easy when taken one step at a time, in the proper order.

Purchasing Thread

Choose your thread wisely. Serging usually uses much more thread than straight-stitching, so it's cost effective to buy larger quantities. Consider quality, color, type of thread, and fiber content before purchasing. If you can't find what you're looking for at your local fabric stores, you can order a wide variety of thread through the mail. (See Reliable Mail-order Sources at the end of this book.)

Serger thread

Serger thread is available on tubes or cones in large quantities of 1,000 to 6,000 yards and is wound to feed from the top for high-speed sewing. It is lighter weight than all-purpose thread so that seams will still be supple, even with several strands of thread in the seam allowance.

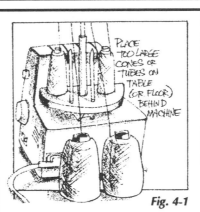

Fig. 4-1

Larger cones or tubes of serger thread may be too big for the spool holder. If so, place them on the table or floor behind the serger. (Fig. 4-1)

Gail Brown

For larger cones of thread, I use a separate cone-thread holder, available at sewing stores or through mail-order sources.

Jan Saunders

✄ **Polyester or nylon thread**—The most widely available serger thread is made of 100% polyester. Both polyester and nylon threads have some elasticity and good strength.

✄ **Cotton-wrapped polyester thread**—A polyester core gives this thread strength and elasticity, while a cotton coating adds heat resistance and blends well with natural-fiber fabrics.

✄ **Cotton thread**—Although it lacks strength and elasticity, cotton thread works well for serging light- and medium-weight natural-fiber fabrics.

✄ **Woolly nylon thread**—This texturized nylon thread comes on cones and makes an especially attractive serger stitch. The unique, crimped texture fluffs out after serging, filling in spaces between the thread for complete coverage of the fabric underneath. (Fig. 4-2)

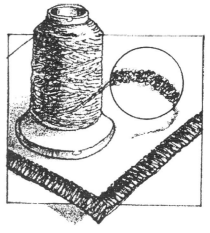

Fig. 4-2: **Texturized woolly nylon has a soft crimp which relaxes after serging and fills in between stitches.**

Because of its texture, woolly nylon has some stretch and works well on stretch fabrics. It is made of 100% nylon and is exceptionally strong. In addition, its soft finish is very comfortable on seams that will be worn next to the skin.

> ***One brand of woolly nylon thread (Talon's Designer Edge) is not crimped. It can be used for all the same purposes and will still fill in between stitches—it just won't fluff out quite as much.***
> ***Naomi Baker***
>
> ***Synthetic threads may leave a sticky residue between the tension discs, and cotton thread may leave lint fibers. Clean the discs regularly (see page 138).***
> ***Jan Saunders***

All-purpose thread

Because of its shorter yardages, all-purpose thread is sometimes less convenient. However, if an exact color match is necessary and you won't be using that color again, you may find it a better buy than large spools or cones of serger thread. All-purpose thread is heavier in weight than serger thread and is best used on medium- to heavy-weight fabrics. Use extra-fine all-purpose thread for more delicate fabrics. When

serging with traditional all-purpose spools, be sure to place the notched side down and use a spool cap for even feeding. (Fig. 4-3)

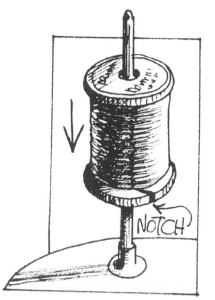

Fig. 4-3: **When serging with all-purpose thread spools, place the notched side down.**

> ***Because of its strength, I always recommend all-purpose thread over lighter weight serger thread.***
> ***Sue Green-Baker***
>
> ***Some imported all-purpose thread is cross-wound in a diamond pattern and will release easily from the top of the spool.***
> ***Gale Grigg Hazen***
>
> ***Look for imported brands of all-purpose thread that come on smooth spools. They won't catch or require spool caps during serging.***
> ***Ruthann Spiegelhoff***

Good quality versus poor quality

Beware of bargains when purchasing thread. The money saved is not worth the frustration of serging with poor-quality thread. Because a serger stitches so quickly—around 1,500 stitches per minute—thread strength and quality are especially important. Inferior thread may have weak spots that break, uneven twists or slubs that catch in a needle or thread guide, or loose fibers that fray.

Look at the thread carefully to judge the quality. Inferior thread, made with short, leftover filaments, may have fiber ends poking out, giving the thread a "hairy" look. Or the thread may be twisted unevenly with thick and thin areas. Quality thread is smooth and evenly twisted. (Fig. 4-4)

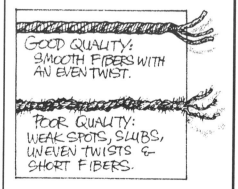

Fig. 4-4: **Purchase only good quality thread to avoid stitching problems.**

Matching or blending?

Purchasing three or four cones or tubes per color of serger thread can be quite costly. You'll be relieved to hear that an exact color match isn't always essential. On 3-thread seams inside a garment, the needle thread is the only thread that might show from the right side. Unless you're stitching sheer fabric or an unlined jacket where the seam allowances will be exposed, it isn't necessary to color-match the looper threads to the garment fabric. When using a 4-thread stitch, use matching thread in the left (seamline) needle.

For blending (rather than matching) serger thread colors, purchase ivory to blend with pastels or light-colored fabrics, gray to blend with medium tones, and black, navy, or brown to blend with darker colors. For an exact color match on small jobs, purchase spools of all-purpose thread.

Decorative options

Serger loopers have much larger eyes than the needles. This allows you to thread them with heavier decorative threads. You'll learn much more about decorative serging in Chapter 12, Looking at Ornamental Options.

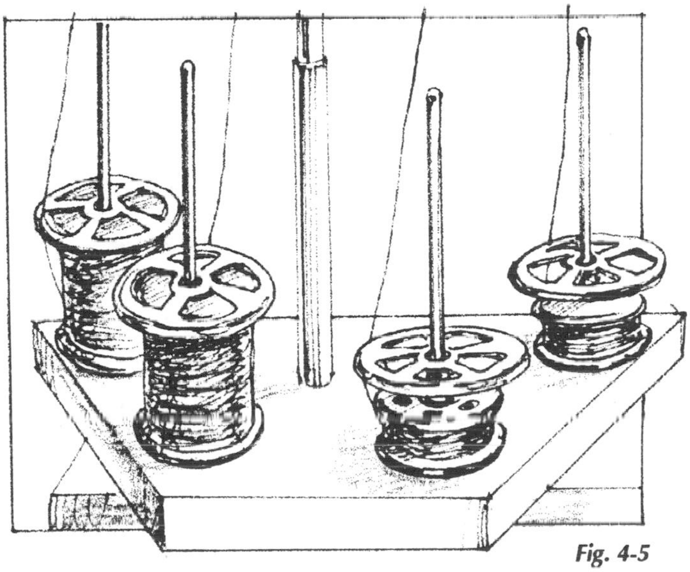

Quick-Change Threading

Experiment with easy quick-change threading. It will save minutes every time you want to change to a different thread type or color. (That can add up to quite a block of precious sewing time!) To use this technique, your serger must already be correctly threaded. If one of the threads is broken or unthreaded, you'll need to rethread from scratch (see The Complete Threading Process, next).

1. Clip the needle thread(s) just above the needle eye(s) and unthread it. You'll need to do this even when the needle thread doesn't need changing. (Fig. 4-6)

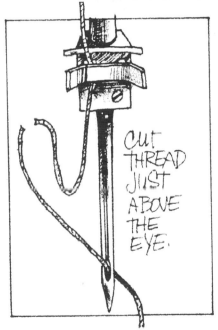

Fig. 4-6: For quick-change threading, always begin by clipping the needle thread.

When you need an obscure thread color for a small garment or project, purchase one or two spools and wind the thread onto spare bobbins. Use the bobbin thread in the needles where less thread is needed, and use the spools or cones for the thread-consuming loopers. (Fig. 4-5)

Ronda Chaney

Fig. 4-5

2. Raise the presser foot. Hold the thread chain behind the presser foot and run the serger until about 4" of unchained thread is stretched behind the needle. The looper threads will separate because the needle thread is clipped. (Fig. 4-7)

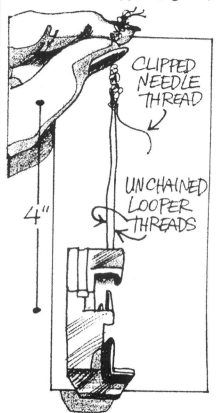

Fig. 4-7: Hold the chain and run the serger to produce 4" of unchained thread.

3. Determine which thread(s) you would like to change and clip each just above the cone or spool. Put new thread onto the spool pin and tie it onto the old thread, pulling at the knot to be sure it's secure before continuing.

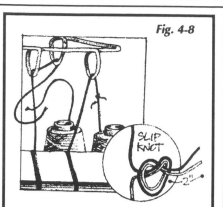

Fig. 4-8

When tying threads, a simple slip knot (technically called an "overhand knot") works well. The key is to leave at least 2" of tail on both threads so the knot will stay tied. (Fig. 4-8)
Sue Green-Baker

4. Remove the thread from the tension discs or turn the dials to their lowest settings. (If your machine has a tension-release lever, hold it down.) This will prevent the knot from untying as you draw the new thread through the machine. Gently pull through each thread that you're replacing (one at a time) until the knot is a few inches behind the presser foot.

5. Rethread the needle(s) and draw the thread down and out under the back of the presser foot. Replace the threads in the tension discs or return the dials to their previous settings. While holding the thread ends behind the presser foot, turn the handwheel a couple of times to be sure the stitches are forming on the stitch finger. Then serge slowly to form a new thread chain.

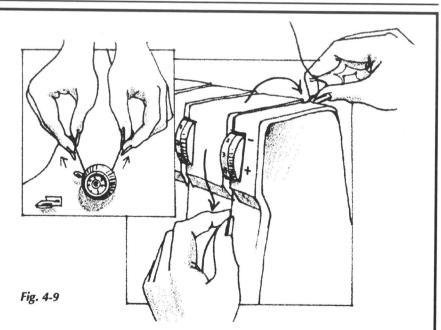

Fig. 4-9

There are two discs inside each tension mechanism. Pressure between these discs places tension on the thread. When rethreading the tension control, tug the thread firmly to be sure it has slipped completely between the discs. (Fig . 4-9) If there is still no tension on the thread, turn the tension dial to the lowest setting, slip the thread between the discs, then return the dial to its previous setting.

Jan Saunders

The Complete Threading Process

To be fully comfortable using your serger, you'll need to practice threading until it's practically second nature to you. Although quick-change threading is very handy, there will be times when you must thread your machine from scratch—especially when a thread breaks or is unthreaded.

Threading from scratch isn't difficult when you work slowly and methodically, but any of us can become frustrated when we try to rush through the process. Follow these guidelines, beginning with a completely unthreaded machine:

✄ Select different thread colors for each spool (see page 15). If your machine has color-coded thread guides, use corresponding thread colors.

✄ Extend the thread-guide pole to its **highest** position, and place the spools or cones on the spool pins.

✄ Consult your owner's manual to determine which looper to thread first. Begin by feeding the end of that thread forward through the initial thread guide(s) on the extended pole. Follow the color-coded thread guides or the diagram on your machine or in the owner's manual. Double-check to be sure the thread has been routed through every guide, and verify that the thread is engaged between the tension discs. (See Fig. 4-9)

✄ Next thread the other looper, following the same procedure you used for the first one. Check to see that the loopers are not crossed before threading the looper eye. If they are, turn the handwheel to position them correctly, as shown. (Fig. 4-11) To verify that the

To ease the threading process, use the threading tools that were supplied with your serger. These usually include tweezers and a looper threader. If a looper threader didn't come with your machine, use a thread cradle or dental floss threader or purchase a wire looper threader. (See Fig. 3-14.)

Sue Green-Baker

I used to rummage around to find my tweezers until I started storing them on the thread-guide pole for easy access. (Fig. 4-10)

Jan Saunders

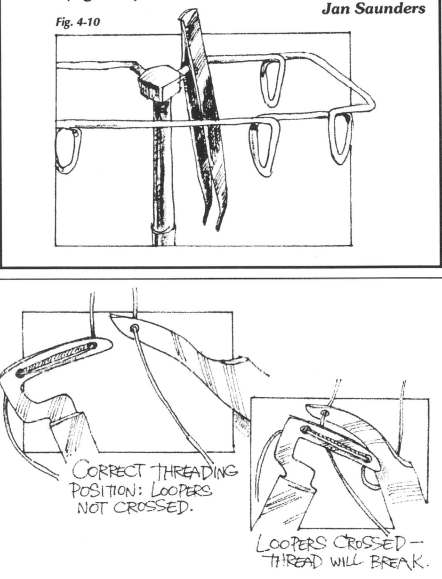

Fig. 4-10

CORRECT THREADING POSITION: LOOPERS NOT CROSSED.

LOOPERS CROSSED— THREAD WILL BREAK.

Fig. 4-11: **Thread the loopers in the uncrossed position.**

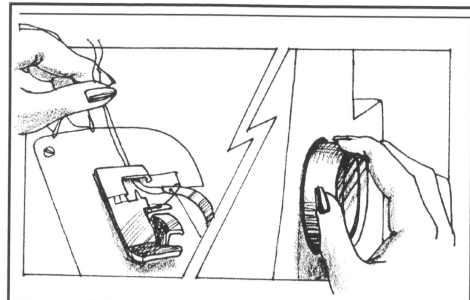

Fig. 4-12: Hold the threads behind the presser foot and turn the handwheel to be sure they won't tangle.

✄ Before beginning to serge, use your tweezers to properly position the thread tails. They should run directly from the looper and needle eyes out under the back of the presser foot. (Fig. 4-13)

✄ Hold the thread ends behind the presser foot, gently guiding them toward the back of the machine while turning the handwheel a few times. Check to be sure stitches are forming on the stitch finger before using the foot control. Serge at least a 3" thread chain, still holding onto (but not pulling) the ends.

loopers are threaded properly and the thread won't tangle, hold the thread ends slightly taut behind the presser foot and turn the handwheel a few times. (Fig. 4-12)

Note: Turn the handwheel in the proper direction. It may turn either counterclockwise, as on a conventional machine, or in the opposite direction. Check the directional arrow on the handwheel or consult your owner's manual for the correct direction.

✄ **Thread the needle(s) last!**
When the needle is threaded before one or both of the loopers, the thread may become trapped and break when you begin to serge. First, feed the thread end through the initial thread guide and follow the color-coded guides or the diagram on your machine or in the owner's manual. Double-check to be sure the thread has been routed through *every* guide, and verify that the thread is engaged between the tension discs before threading the needle.

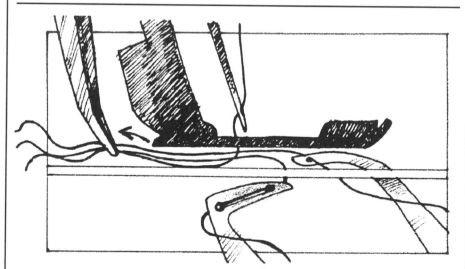

Fig. 4-13: Before serging, draw the threads out under the back of the foot.

Threading Trouble-shooting

If the thread keeps breaking, or stitches are not forming properly, or a thread chain is not forming at all, chances are the serger is threaded incorrectly—the most common serger problem. The solution is relatively simple: carefully retrace the thread paths, one at a time:

1. Begin tracing each thread at the spool base. Is the thread unwinding smoothly from the cone or spool? Make certain the thread-guide pole is extended to its highest position. And be sure the thread is not wrapped around the spool pin, caught in a spool notch, or wound under the spool. For even feeding, use spool caps or cone holders.

> *On several models, the spool base must be moved to the right and clicked into position for serging (check your owner's manual setup procedure). Not moving it over will cause incorrect stitching.*
> *Gale Grigg Hazen*

2. Unwind a yard of thread by hand from the cone or spool to see if the thread is unreeling freely and evenly. If it isn't, check for excess glue from the wrapper or possibly a drop of seam sealant. Unwind and discard the unusable thread.

3. Continue tracing each thread path to be sure every guide has been threaded, including the eye of the looper or needle. Also make certain the thread is not wrapped around any guides twice or threaded through in the wrong direction. Check that the thread is not wrapped around the needle. (Fig. 4-14)

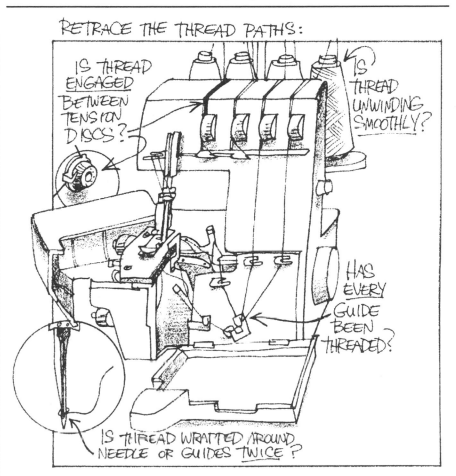

Fig. 4-14: **When you have a threading problem, check the most common reasons.**

4. Tug the thread into the tension mechanism to be sure it is securely between the discs. (See Fig. 4-9)

5. Position the thread tails directly from the looper and needle eyes out under the back of the presser foot. (See Fig. 4-12)

6. If you're still having problems, clip the needle thread(s) just above the eye, and turn the handwheel until the loopers are not crossing. (See Fig. 4-11) Hold the threads behind the presser foot and turn the handwheel a few times to confirm that they are properly threaded before rethreading the needle(s).

7. If you still can't thread the machine properly, get a good night's sleep and start again when you're fresh and not frustrated. Completely rethread from scratch, following the sequence recommended in your owner's manual.

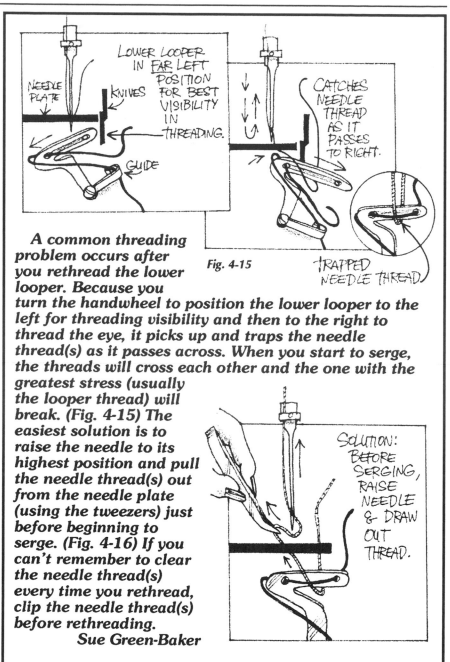

Fig. 4-15

Fig. 4-16

A common threading problem occurs after you rethread the lower looper. Because you turn the handwheel to position the lower looper to the left for threading visibility and then to the right to thread the eye, it picks up and traps the needle thread(s) as it passes across. When you start to serge, the threads will cross each other and the one with the greatest stress (usually the looper thread) will break. (Fig. 4-15) The easiest solution is to raise the needle to its highest position and pull the needle thread(s) out from the needle plate (using the tweezers) just before beginning to serge. (Fig. 4-16) If you can't remember to clear the needle thread(s) every time you rethread, clip the needle thread(s) before rethreading.
Sue Green-Baker

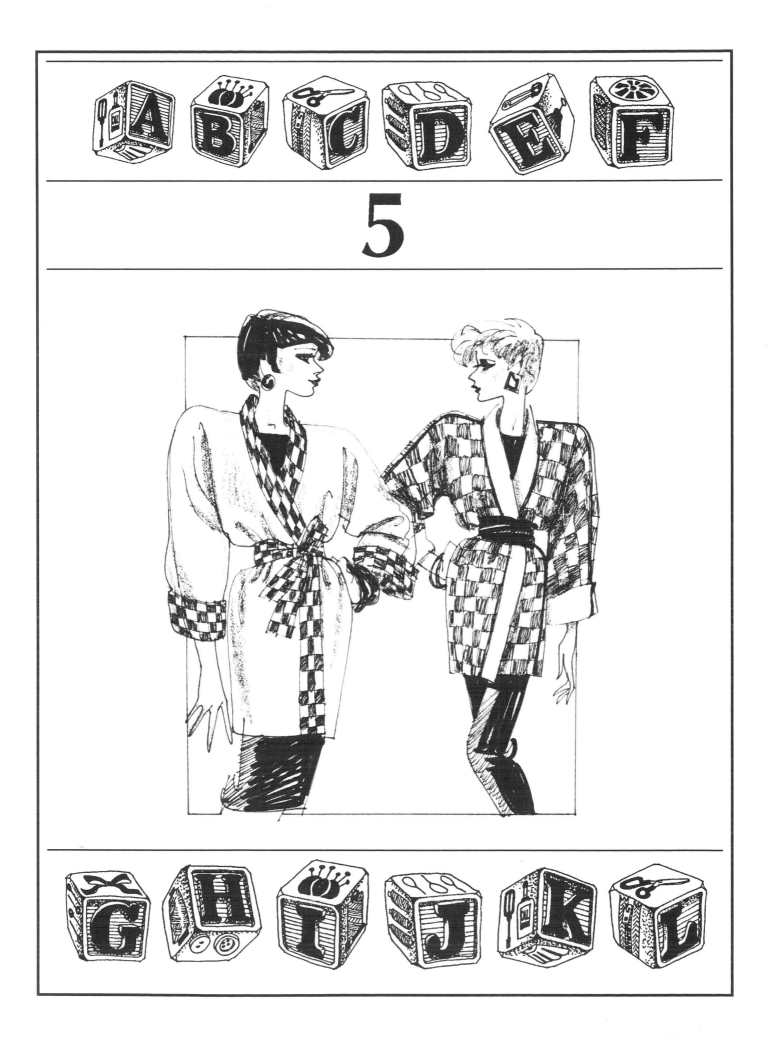

5

njoying Your First Stitches

Getting Started

Now that you've properly threaded your machine, it's time to begin serging. At this point, simply leave your tension dials and width adjustments at the manufacturer's settings. The tension is usually properly adjusted at the factory. If your serger hasn't come directly from a dealer or you're uncertain about the adjustments, simply turn the tension dials to the center settings. The tension may not be perfect, but don't worry about it now. We'll discuss those adjustments in later chapters.

Safe serging

Learn a few essential safety tips before you begin stitching: (Fig. 5-1)

✄ As with a conventional sewing machine, **it's essential to keep your fingers away from the needle(s).** Some serger models come equipped with a needle guard to help protect against stitched fingers. On the others, use the same caution you would for any sewing machine needle.

✄ **Also beware of the knives.** All sergers have a knife guard, but it's still possible to get too close. Keep your fingers away from the knife area while the serger is operating.

✄ **Turn off the power** when cleaning, oiling, changing knives or other parts, and any time you step away from the machine.

✄ **Do not pull the fabric through the machine** when

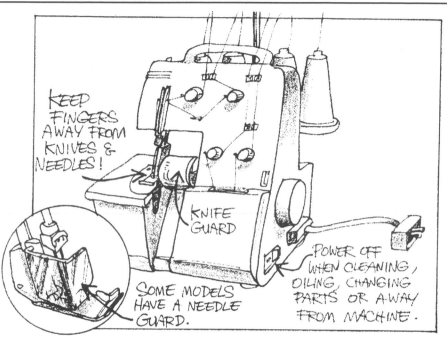

Fig. 5-1: Sergers are designed for safety, but you must follow basic precautions.

serging, because the needle could bend and hit a looper. This can cause a broken needle, or worse, the serger could be damaged or thrown out of alignment. Once the fabric is under the presser foot, the feed dogs draw it along—there's no need to pull.

Fig. 5-2

I often suggest holding the fabric taut while serging. This takes the slack out of it as it's being fed through by the machine so stitches will form smoothly. But note: do not pull it through from the back faster than the feed dogs are moving. (Fig. 5-2)

Naomi Baker

Serging a thread chain

In the last chapter, you threaded your serger and produced a short thread chain. Unlike a conventional sewing machine, the serger's stitches will loop together to form a chain, even when fabric is not being used. On a serger, the only way to "pull the threads" and remove the fabric when you're finished stitching is to serge a chain.

> *A few serger models have a tension-release feature, so it isn't always necessary to chain off. Check your owner's manual.*
> **Jan Saunders**

To practice, continue serging the thread chain you began in Chapter 4, holding onto the chain with your left hand until you have about 10". Clip off part of the chain, leaving about 3" on the machine.

Basic Driving Skills

There are a number of things you should know before you begin serging on fabric. Because a serger is different from a conventional sewing machine, you'll need to relearn some basic skills for guiding the fabric (or "driving" the serger).

The knives

A serger has two knives or cutters that work together like scissors to trim the fabric. If your serger's knife can be disengaged, be sure it is in the cutting position now. The knives cut the fabric approximately 3/4" ahead of the needle. (Fig. 5-3) As a result, the

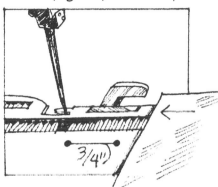

Fig. 5-3: **The fabric is cut 3/4" before the needle forms stitches.**

fabric is cut well before it is stitched. Unlike a stitching error, a cut in the fabric cannot be corrected, so guide carefully.

To maintain a neat, even seam allowance, always guide the fabric so you're trimming at least a slight amount off the edge as you serge. It's easiest to trim between 1/8" and 3/8", but just skimming the edge to neaten it will produce the same effect.

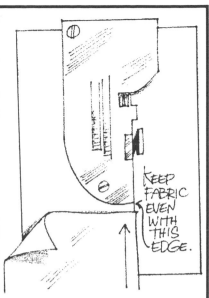

Fig. 5-4

> *The right side of the throat plate is usually aligned with the cutting blades. If you hold the fabric even with it, the serger will just skim and neaten the edge.*
> **Gale Grigg Hazen**

Judging the stitching line

The stitching line (or the seamline when seaming two layers of fabric) is the point at which the needle enters the fabric. If you're serging with two needles, it is the point where the left needle enters the fabric.

It's often difficult to see the stitching line because of the shape of the presser foot. It's also difficult to watch the needle and the knives at the same time. For the most accurate serging, mark the needleline(s) on the top and front of the presser foot using a fine-tipped permanent marker. When you serge, guide the fabric so the desired stitching line is aligned with the needleline mark on the presser foot. (Fig. 5-5)

a 1/4" stitch width, you'll trim off 3/8" to position the needle on the seamline. (Fig. 5-6)

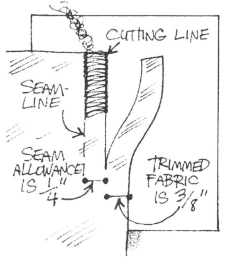

Fig. 5-6: The serged seam allowance is the distance between the seamline and the cutting line.

Some models have markings on the knife guard or machine door that show where to guide the raw edge of a 5/8" seam allowance. If your serger doesn't have these markings, measure from the stitching line 5/8" to the right, where the raw edge should be guided. Place a piece of masking tape on the machine and mark the guideline on the tape, or use a fine-tipped permanent marker and mark the line directly onto the machine. (Fig. 5-7) Also mark other seam allowance widths you'll use, such as 1/2", 3/4", and 1".

An attractive, professionally printed measuring decal for guiding your fabric edge is available through mail-order sources.

Jan Saunders

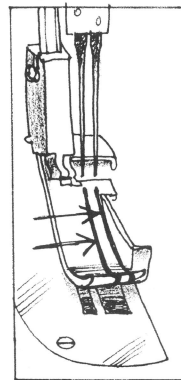

Fig. 5-5: Mark the needleline(s) on the top and front of the presser foot.

Guiding the seam allowance

You won't always want to guide your fabric by the stitching line because it may not be easy to recognize on your fabric. Instead, it is often easier to guide the raw edge of the fabric.

If the width of your serged stitch is about 5mm or 1/4" and you've cut a garment with 1/4" seam allowances, just guide the edge of the fabric along the side of the knife. If your allowances are 5/8", you'll need to guide the fabric so part is trimmed off and the rest is in the seam allowance. For example, with a 5/8" allowance and

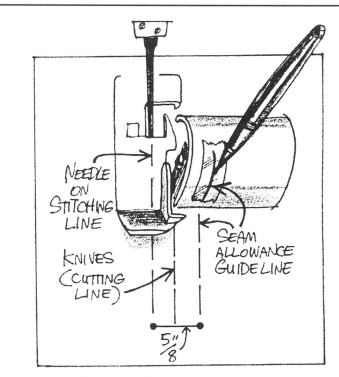

Fig. 5-7: Mark seam allowance guidelines on the knife guard or door 5/8" from the stitching line.

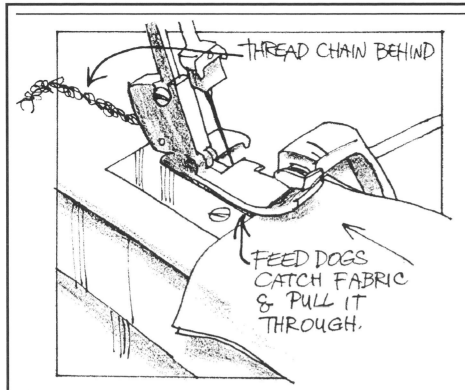

THREAD CHAIN BEHIND

FEED DOGS CATCH FABRIC & PULL IT THROUGH.

Fig. 5-8: There's often no need to lift the presser foot when beginning to serge. Simply position the fabric under the front of the foot.

When you're serging thick, slippery, or stretchy fabric, or when matching a stripe or plaid, lift the presser foot first. Position the fabric under the foot, just in front of the knives. (Be sure the thread chain is still feeding out under the back.) Then lower the foot and begin serging.

Test Stitching

It's now time to practice your driving skills. Use any mediumweight fabric scraps and practice until you feel comfortable. The stitch may not look perfect, but you'll learn to adjust it in the next couple of chapters.

Stitching onto fabric

Serge a 3" thread chain and position the chain under and behind the presser foot. It may be unnecessary to lift the presser foot when serging onto fabric. Simply place the front edge of the fabric under the front of the presser foot. The feed dogs will catch it and guide it through. (Fig. 5-8)

> *I always lift at least the toe of the foot when feeding in the fabric. If not, the layers can shift slightly.*
> *Sue Green-Baker*

Guiding the fabric

Place your left hand palm down, flat on the fabric, positioned on the bed of the machine to the left and slightly in back of the needles. (Fig. 5-9) With your right hand, hold the edge of the fabric, guiding it into the machine.

> *Always allow the machine to pull the fabric into the machine, so the knives can do their job. If you raise the foot and push in too much fabric, the blades won't cut all of it, creating a jam.*
> *Gale Grigg Hazen*

Note: The feed dogs will draw the fabric through, so there's no need to pull it.

Chaining off

After you've serged to the end of the fabric, continue stitching, forming 5" to 6" of thread chain off the edge. This is referred to as "chaining off." Using thread clips or scissors, clip the chain, freeing the fabric and leaving about 3" of chain on the serger. (Fig. 5-10) In Chapter 9, you'll learn how to secure the end of the serging so it won't ravel. For now, though, just chain off.

> *Even if someone has demonstrated serging over your thread chain to cut it off, it's not a good habit. The chain can get caught in the loopers.*
> *Naomi Baker*

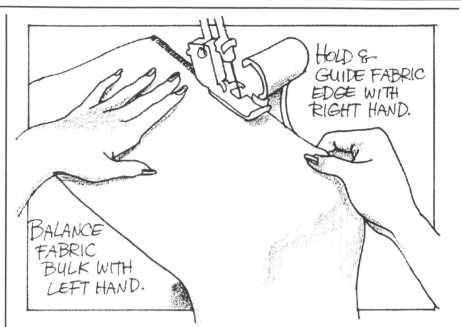

HOLD & GUIDE FABRIC EDGE WITH RIGHT HAND.

BALANCE FABRIC BULK WITH LEFT HAND.

Fig. 5-9: Guide the fabric with both hands.

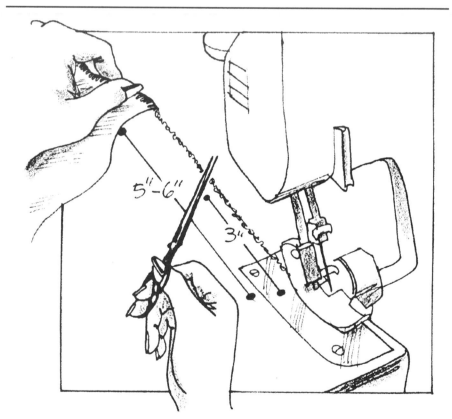

5"-6"

3"

Fig. 5-10: Chain off for 5" or 6". Then clip the chain, leaving 3" connected to the serger.

6

Focusing on Tension

✂ **Understanding Tension**
✂ **Balanced 3- and 4-thread Overlock Tension**
✂ **Balanced 2-thread Overedge Tension**
✂ **Balanced Chainstitch Tension**
✂ **Practicing Tension Adjustment**
✂ **Tips for Balancing Tension**

Understanding Tension

Changing the tension settings is a basic and essential serging skill. Unlike the tension on your sewing machine, serger tension may need adjustment when you change your stitch width or length, fabric, or thread type. Proficiency at fine-tuning serger tensions can make a major difference in the stitch results and, in turn, the quality of your final garment or project.

Tension controls can be in the form of round knobs on the front of the machine or vertical slots and inset dials near the top of the machine. (See Fig. 2-8) No matter which type you have, there are two discs inside each tension mechanism. As the thread feeds between the discs, the pressure between them puts tension on the thread. By adjusting the knob or dial, you increase or reduce the pressure. (See page 30 for tips on threading the tension mechanism.)

> *If your serger has round knobs rather than inset dials, use the playful jingle "righty-tighty, lefty-loosey" to easily remember which direction to turn the dial when tightening or loosening the tension. This works for most of the machine's other knobs and screws, too.*
> **Sue Green-Baker**

Tension adjustment not only will perfect a balanced stitch, but also can be used in creating stitch variations, such as the flatlock stitch you'll learn in Chapter 13 and the rolled edge stitch we'll introduce in Chapter 14.

Balanced 3- and 4-thread Overlock Tension

When the tension is correctly adjusted for a balanced 3- or 4-thread stitch, the looper threads lie evenly on the top and underside of the fabric, interlocking exactly at the fabric edge. Before beginning to adjust the tension, it's important to know what a correctly adjusted stitch looks like. Examine the illustrations as you read the tension descriptions. (Fig. 6-1)

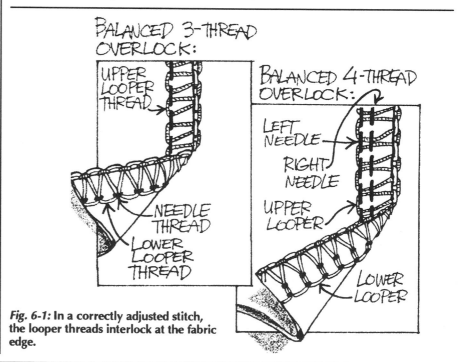

Fig. 6-1: In a correctly adjusted stitch, the looper threads interlock at the fabric edge.

Needle tension

The needle thread (the left needle on a 4-thread stitch) runs along the stitching line or the seamline. On a balanced stitch, it resembles a line of straight-stitching on top of the fabric, with small loops peeking through to the underside.

The needle-thread tension control will affect the stitch only at the seamline. If the tension is too loose, the thread will form larger loops on the underside and the seam will spread apart when pulled. (Fig. 6-2) If the tension is too tight, the fabric will pucker at the seamline. (Fig. 6-3)

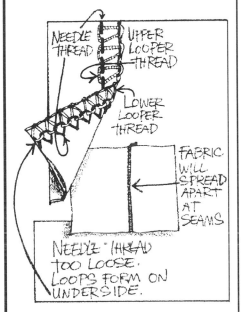

Fig. 6-2: When the needle thread tension is too loose, the seamline pulls apart.

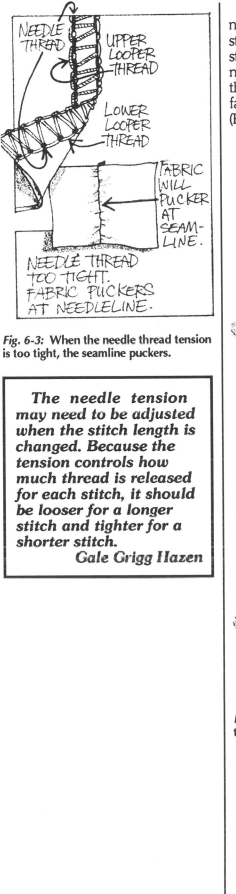

Fig. 6-3: When the needle thread tension is too tight, the seamline puckers.

> *The needle tension may need to be adjusted when the stitch length is changed. Because the tension controls how much thread is released for each stitch, it should be looser for a longer stitch and tighter for a shorter stitch.*
> **Gale Grigg Hazen**

On a 4-thread stitch, the right needle thread forms a line of stitching down the center of the stitch. Adjust it to look like the left needle thread. Loops will form if the tension is too loose, and the fabric will pucker if it is too tight. (Fig. 6-4)

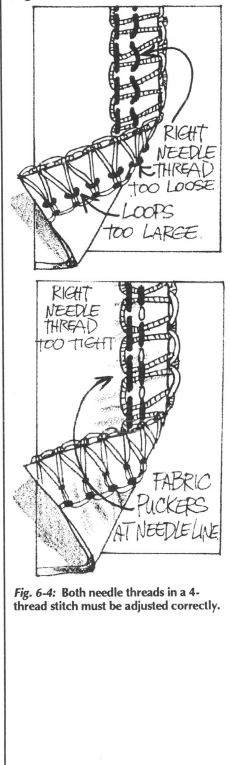

Fig. 6-4: Both needle threads in a 4-thread stitch must be adjusted correctly.

Looper tensions

In a balanced stitch, the upper looper thread forms loops on the topside of the fabric and the lower looper thread forms loops on the underside of the fabric. When the tension is correctly adjusted, the threads should lie flat, interlocking with the needle thread on the seamline and with each other on the cut edge of the fabric.

Often when the stitch isn't correctly balanced, it is because one of the looper tensions is too tight. When the upper looper tension is too tight, it will pull the lower looper thread around the fabric edge to the topside and may cause the fabric to roll or bunch. (Fig. 6-5) When the lower looper tension is too tight, it will similarly pull the upper looper thread to the underside of the fabric. (Fig. 6-6)

One or both of the looper tensions might be too loose. If so, the stitches will wrap to the opposite side of the fabric or will hang off the edge. (Fig. 6-7)

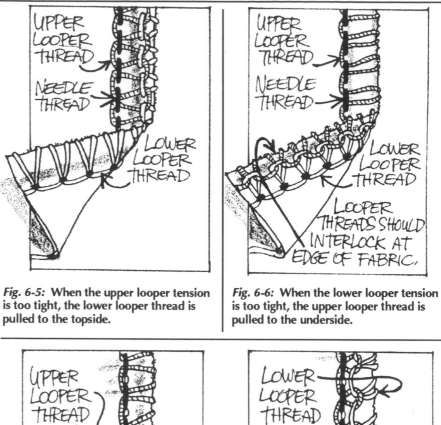

Fig. 6-5: When the upper looper tension is too tight, the lower looper thread is pulled to the topside.

Fig. 6-6: When the lower looper tension is too tight, the upper looper thread is pulled to the underside.

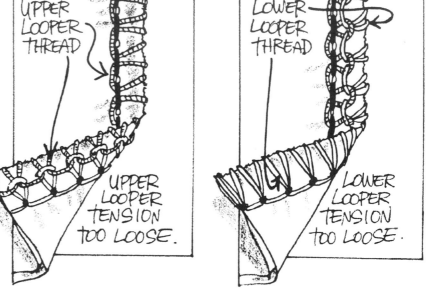

Fig. 6-7: When a looper tension is too loose, the thread will wrap to the opposite side.

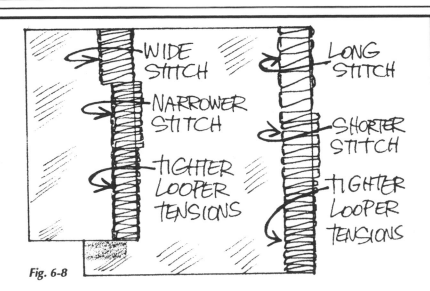

Fig. 6-8

When the stitch width or length is changed, the looper tensions may need adjustment. A narrower stitch or shorter stitch needs less thread, so it requires tighter looper tensions. A wider or longer stitch requires looser looper tensions because more thread is needed to cover the expanded distance. (Fig. 6-8) A variation in fabric thickness may also require looper tension adjustment. Thick fabric needs more thread to go around the fabric edge, so you'll need to loosen the looper tensions. For thin fabric, you'll need less thread, so tighten the tensions.

Gale Grigg Hazen

Balanced 2-thread Overedge Tension

The 2-thread overedge stitch has one needle thread and one looper thread. (Fig. 6-9) The looper thread lies on top of the fabric and interlocks with the needle thread at both the stitching line and the fabric edge, similar to the upper looper thread in a 3-thread stitch. The needle thread forms a line of stitching on the topside of the fabric. On the underside, it extends to the fabric edge.

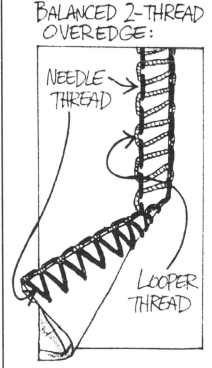

BALANCED 2-THREAD OVEREDGE:

NEEDLE THREAD

LOOPER THREAD

Fig. 6-9: In a balanced 2-thread overedge stitch, the needle thread interlocks with the looper thread on both sides of the stitch.

If the looper thread is too tight, it will pull the needle thread over the edge to the topside and the fabric may roll or bunch. If the needle thread is too tight, it will similarly pull the looper thread to the underside. (Fig. 6-10)

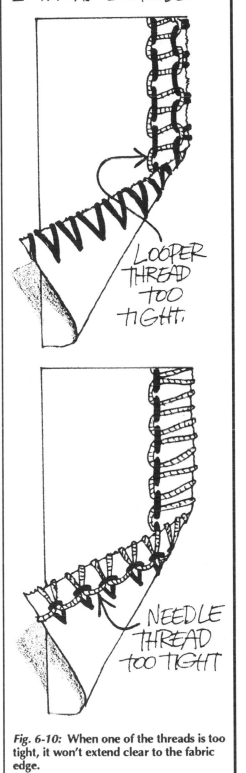

2-THREAD OVEREDGE:

LOOPER THREAD TOO TIGHT.

NEEDLE THREAD TOO TIGHT

Fig. 6-10: When one of the threads is too tight, it won't extend clear to the fabric edge.

When the tension on either the looper or needle thread is too loose, that thread will wrap loosely and unevenly to the opposite side of the fabric.

Balanced Chainstitch Tension

The chainstitch consists of one needle thread and one looper thread. From the topside, this stitch looks similar to a conventional straight-stitch. From the underside, the chain is visible. (Fig. 6-11)

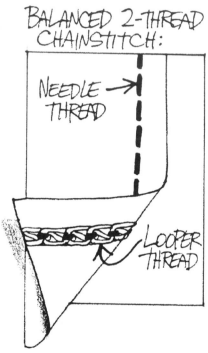

BALANCED 2-THREAD CHAINSTITCH:

NEEDLE THREAD →

LOOPER THREAD

Fig. 6-11: A balanced 2-thread chainstitch will lie smoothly on both sides of the fabric.

> *On a chainstitch, you usually won't need to adjust the tension, especially not the needle tension.*
> **Naomi Baker**

If one or both tensions are too tight, the seam will pucker or will unravel because of skipped stitches. If the tensions are too loose, the stitching will look looped and uneven.

> *Also use different thread colors to practice the chainstitch so you can easily see which thread is too loose or too tight.*
> **Ruthann Spiegelhoff**

Practicing Tension Adjustment

Now that you know how to recognize balanced and unbalanced tension, we recommend that you try turning the controls to their limits to see the full effect of changing the settings.

1. Cut long, 4"-wide strips of fabric. You'll be able to serge, stop and adjust, and serge again down the length of the strip without having to serge on and off small scraps of fabric.

2. Thread your serger for a 3-thread stitch, using different colors of thread in each position. (If you have color-coded thread guides, use thread colors to match.)

3. Find the center or normal setting for all the tensions. If the tension dials don't have numbers, try setting them as close to the center as possible.

4. Begin serging the edge of one of the long fabric strips, and slowly turn the lower looper tension all the way to the left (or the lowest and loosest setting). Examine the results to learn what the lower looper thread looks like when the tension is at its loosest setting.

5. Continue serging, readjusting the lower looper tension to the highest (tightest) setting. (The upper looper and needle tensions are still at their center settings.) Examine the results.

6. When the fabric strip runs out, continue serging onto another strip. Label the sections of each strip to identify the various tension adjustments.

7. Turn the lower looper tension back to the center or normal position and the upper looper tension to its lowest (loosest) setting. Serge a section of the strip and examine the results.

8. Repeat step 7, turning the upper looper to the highest (tightest) setting. Continue to label your serging sample.

9. Readjust the upper looper to the center or normal position, then tighten and loosen the needle tension, examining the results after each adjustment. Label the sample.

10. Examine and compare the sample sections with the various tension adjustment illustrations in this chapter.

> *Don't forget to keep samples and record your tension settings for a notebook, note cards, or a bulletin board chart.*
> **Jan Saunders**

Tips for Balancing Tension

✂ While practicing, use different thread colors, matching the color-coded thread guides on your machine (if you have them).

> *Make sure you use the same thread weight, fiber, and twist while adjusting for basic settings. If they are all different, they'll pull against each other with different resistance and give you false readings. The best way to know they're the same is to use the same brand.*
> *Gale Grigg Hazen*

✂ Begin by setting all the tension controls to the center or normal settings.

✂ If your machine isn't marked and you tend to forget which tension control adjusts which thread, label each on a small piece of masking tape. Remove the labels when you've mastered the tension positions.

✂ When testing, use long, single-layer strips of 4"-wide fabric. Stitch a few inches, examine the results, make adjustments, and stitch again. Continue this procedure until the stitch is perfected.

✂ Adjust one dial at a time and test-serge after each adjustment. (If you change more than one tension at a time, you won't know which adjustment produced the results.)

✂ If an adjustment doesn't improve the stitch or worsens it, put the tension control back to its original setting.

✂ Make small adjustments. A fractional change can often make major differences in the stitch.

✂ Loosen the looper tensions after widening the stitch. Tighten them after narrowing the stitch.

✂ Loosen the looper tensions after lengthening the stitch. Tighten them after shortening the stitch.

✂ Use looser tensions with thicker fabric or multiple layers and tighter tensions with thinner fabric or fewer layers.

> *It's not always accurate to refer to tension settings by the number on the dial. The tension controls are hand-calibrated for each machine. As a result, the actual tension between the discs on a particular setting may vary from one machine (even the same model) to another or on the same machine over a period of time.*
> *Gale Grigg Hazen*

✂ Heavier threads often require looser tensions, while finer or more slippery threads require tighter tensions. When adjusting the tension for unusual thread, consider the textural resistance of the thread between the tension discs. A rough, more textured thread will require a looser tension, while a smooth thread will require a tighter tension.

> *Especially after different repair persons work on your serger, the tension calibrations may change.*
> *Ronda Chaney*

7

Getting a Handle on Stitch Sizes

✄ **Regulating Stitch Length**
✄ **Regulating Stitch Width**

As with your conventional sewing machine, your serger's stitch width and length are adjustable. Because each serger model is different, refer to your owner's manual for the adjustment procedures for your machine.

Regulating Stitch Length

Stitch length refers to the distance between needleholes from one stitch to the next. (Fig. 7-1) It is usually measured in millimeters and ranges from less than 1mm to approximately 5mm. (The length capability may vary from one model to another.)

> *I refer to the stitch length as the length of the needleline straight-stitch. The numbers are read the same as on a sewing machine—1 is short and 5 is long.*
> **Sue Green-Baker**

Adjustment tips

Length adjustments vary with the serger model but are usually made by turning a knob or lever.

The length adjustment control may be located outside the machine or inside the cover. If the control is on the outside, you can adjust the length while serging. On some models, you'll need to hold the handwheel while adjusting the length; or turn the handwheel to a certain position, then adjust the length. (Fig. 7-2) *Refer to your owner's manual for specifics.*

Practice adjusting the stitch length. Make the stitch as long and as short as possible. Experiment by serging a sample of each.

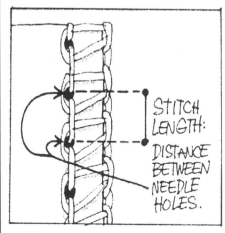

Fig. 7-1: The stitch length measurement is determined at the needleline.

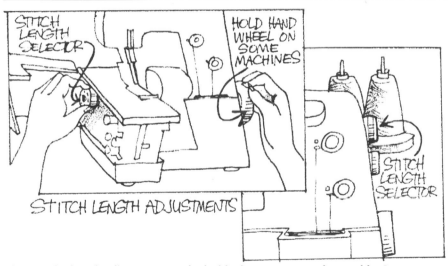

Fig. 7-2: The length adjustment may be inside the cover or on the outside. Some models require that you hold the handwheel while adjusting the length.

Length guidelines

✂ Always test on the same fabric and number of layers you will be using for your garment or project.

> **Before beginning a garment, also test the fabric layers on all grains—usually lengthwise, crosswise, and bias are all serged. This is especially important if the serging will be exposed on the outside of your garment.**
> **Ronda Chaney**

✂ An average or "normal" stitch length (some machines have an "N" marked on the adjustment control) is 3mm (about 10 stitches per inch).

✂ In general, use longer stitches for heavier fabric and shorter stitches on lightweight fabric. A long stitch may cause lighter-weight fabrics to pucker. (Fig. 7-3)

> **I suggest that my students write these sentences on a 3 x 5 card and post it in front of their machine: If the fabric puckers, shorten the stitch. If the fabric waves out of shape, lengthen the stitch. Shortening the stitch holds the fabric flatter; lengthening it keeps it from stretching out of shape.**
> **Jan Saunders**

✂ When serging stiff or delicate fabrics (such as taffeta or chiffon), too short a stitch length may create so many needle holes that the stitch pulls away from the fabric. Use a longer stitch.

✂ When serging knits or bias edges, too short a stitch may cause the edge to stretch, so use a longer stitch. (Fig. 7-3)

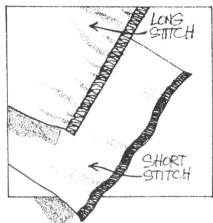

Fig. 7-3: **A long stitch may cause lightweight fabrics to pucker. A short stitch may cause knits or bias fabrics to stretch.**

✂ If necessary, adjust the looper tensions after changing the stitch length. A longer stitch will require looser tensions and a shorter stitch, tighter tensions. (Refer back to Chapter 6 for more information on tension adjustment.)

✂ If the stitch is too short, the fabric may jam under the presser foot. To avoid this problem, especially when using heavier decorative threads, always begin with an average or medium-length stitch and shorten it a little at a time until you reach the length desired. The stitch length on a serger is changed for the same reasons you change it on a sewing machine.

> **Remember the length as the straight-stitch in the seamline. The width is the zigzag of the overcast stitches.**
> **Sue Green-Baker**

Regulating Stitch Width

Stitch width refers to the distance between the needleholes (the left needleholes on a 4- or 5-thread stitch) and the cut edge. (Fig. 7-4) It is measured in millimeters and can range from 1.5mm to 9mm, depending on the stitch type and the serger model.

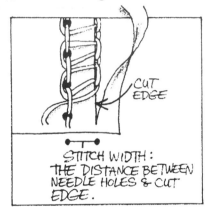

Fig. 7-4: **The stitch width is measured from the needleline to the cut edge.**

Adjustment tips

The stitch width adjustment procedure varies widely from model to model. We've generalized the differences into three categories and given tips for each type of adjustment. However, it's important to *refer to your owner's manual for exact procedures.*

✂ **Varying the needle position**—On most sergers with a 4-thread overlock stitch you have the option of using either the left or right needle position for the 3-thread stitch. Remove one needle and use the right needle only for a narrow 3-thread stitch or the left needle only for a wide 3-thread stitch. (Fig. 7-5)

✂ **Adjusting the cutting width**—On many machines you can adjust the stitch width by changing the lower-knife position. This adjusts the width at which the fabric is cut, so the looper threads wrap over and under a wider edge.

Some machines have an adjustment knob and others have a screw—check your owner's manual to be sure. If your width adjustment isn't automatic, you may need to disengage the upper knife and adjust the lower knife position. (Fig. 7-6) When finished, reengage the upper knife; it will automatically align with the lower one.

Note: If it is not a standard adjustment on your machine, we do not recommend moving the lower knife—it can be difficult to position properly. If you're uncertain about this adjustment, check with your local dealer.

✂ **Changing the stitch finger**—On many machines you can convert to a narrower stitch by changing or adjusting the stitch finger. Because the looper threads form around the stitch finger, a wider stitch finger will result in wider stitches.

Changing the stitch finger may require changing the needle plate or the presser foot where the stitch finger is located. Some models have an adjustment that conveniently widens or narrows the stitch finger, and others have an easily removable stitch finger (see Fig. 2-9).

Note: Many machines have a combination of the above options. A 4-thread overlock model, for example, often has a cutting width adjustment in addition to the ability to stitch with either needle.

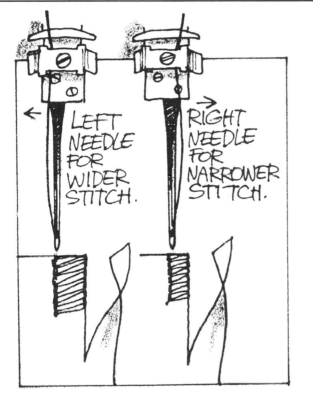

Fig. 7-5: Changing the needle position is one way to vary the stitch width.

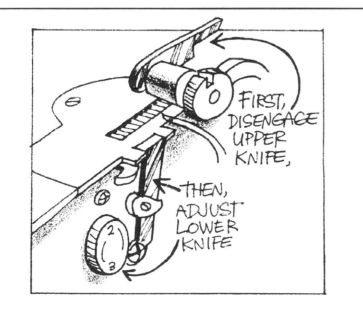

Fig. 7-6: Move the lower knife to change the cutting width.

Width Guidelines

✄ Heavy fabrics need a wider stitch for durability and so the seam allowance will press flat. Use a slightly narrower stitch for lightweight fabrics. They may roll or bunch under a too-wide stitch. (Fig. 7-7)

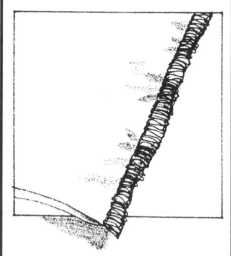

Fig. 7-7: Lightweight fabrics may roll or bunch in the seam allowance when the stitch is too wide.

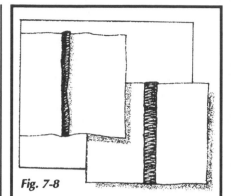

Fig. 7-8

If the seam allowances won't press flat, try widening the stitch. Most heavy fabrics should be serged using your widest stitch. (Fig. 7-8)
Gail Brown

✄ A wide stitch is more durable for ravelly fabrics. For sheer or lightweight fabrics, loosen the looper tensions on a wide stitch to help prevent the fabric from bunching under the serging.

If you have a 3-thread serger without a wide-width stitch option, you may need to use a straight-stitch to keep heavier fabric seams flat.
Ruthann Spiegelhoff

✄ Readjust the looper tensions after changing the stitch width. Use looser tensions for a wider stitch and tighter tensions for a narrower stitch. (See Chapter 6 for tips on adjusting tension.)

WRAPPED CORNERS:

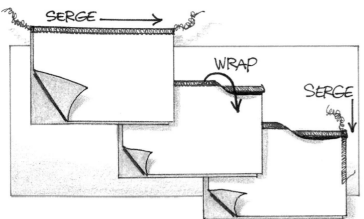

SERGE →

WRAP

SERGE

For perfect corner points, serge-seam one side. Press the seam flat, then fold and press again, wrapping the seam allowance toward the garment. Serge the adjoining side, stitching over the folded allowance. Turn right side out and press again.

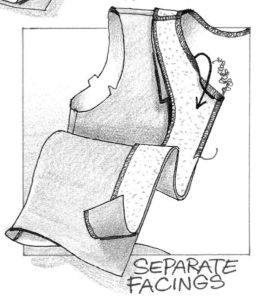

WRAP OUTER EDGES, THEN SERGE SIDES.

2-PIECE CUFFS

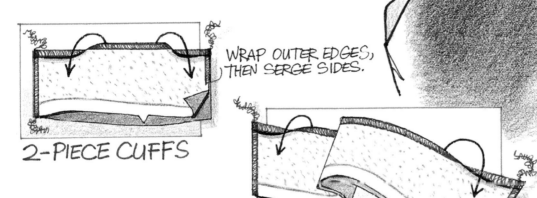

2-PIECE COLLARS

WRAP NECKLINE EDGE, THEN SERGE FRONT EDGE.

WRAP TOP & BOTTOM, THEN SERGE SIDES.

LEAVE OPENING FOR TURNING.

LINED PATCH POCKETS

SEPARATE FACINGS

SERGED IN-SEAM POCKET:

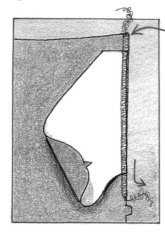

SERGE-SEAM WITHOUT TRIMMING.

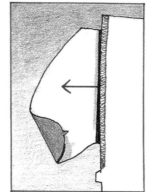

With right sides together, serge the pocket pieces to the garment. Serge-seam without trimming so the stitching is along the outer edge of the seam allowances.

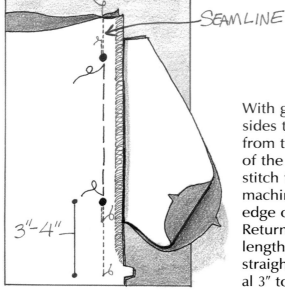

SEAMLINE

3"–4"

With garment sections right sides together, straight-stitch from the waistline to the top of the pocket opening. Back-stitch to secure, then machine-baste to the lower edge of the pocket opening. Return to a normal stitch length, back-stitch again, and straight-stitch for an additional 3" to 4".

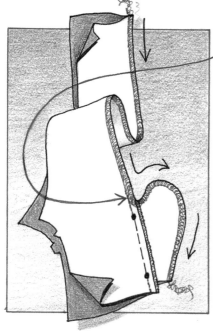

SERGE-SEAM WITH NEEDLE ON SEAMLINE.

Beginning at the hemline, serge-seam the sides. When you reach the lower pocket edge, gently angle toward the pocket seamline, pulling it out in front of the presser foot in a straight line (see Chapter 10 for more information on inside corners and angles). Continue serge-seaming around the outside pocket edge. Press the pocket toward the front, finish the waistline edge, and carefully remove the machine basting at the opening.

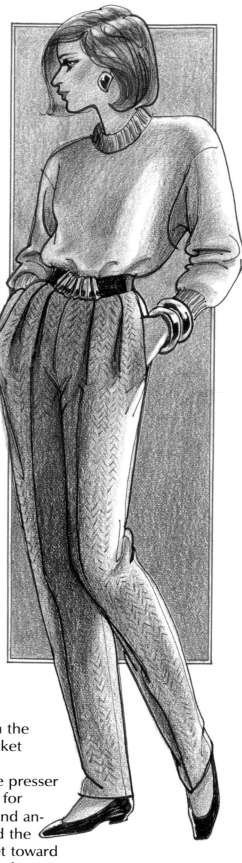

SIMPLE PULL-ON WAISTBAND:

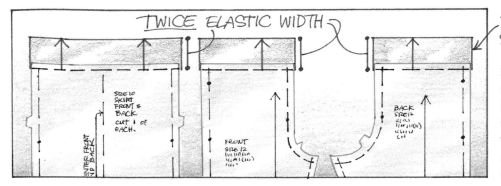

TWICE ELASTIC WIDTH

EXTEND WAISTLINE SEAM ALLOWANCE.

SIZE 10 SKIRT FRONT & BACK CUT 1 OF EACH.

CENTER FRONT OR BACK

FRONT SIZE 12

BACK SIZE 12

Select 1¼" to 1½" wide, sew-through elastic for a basic pull-on skirt or pant. Cut out the garment with a waistline seam allowance double the width of the elastic.

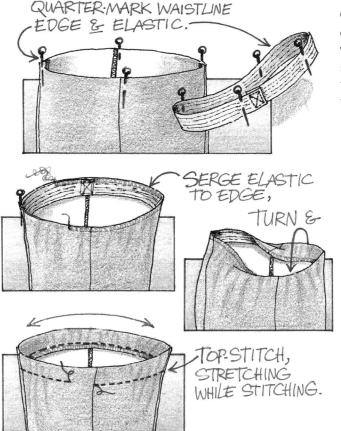

QUARTER-MARK WAISTLINE EDGE & ELASTIC.

SERGE ELASTIC TO EDGE, TURN &

TOP-STITCH, STRETCHING WHILE STITCHING.

Complete the garment except for the waistline edge. Fit the elastic comfortably around the waist (about 2" less than the measurement), then straight-stitch or zigzag the overlapped ends to form a circle. Mark four equal sections on both the waistline edge and elastic.

With the elastic on top, serge-seam the elastic to the edge, matching the quartermarks. Turn the elastic to the inside and straight-stitch in place along the serging needleline, stretching as you sew. Stitch-in-the-ditch at the side seams to keep the elastic from rolling. For detailed garment construction information, see Chapter 15.

SERGED SEAMS

BASIC SEAMS:

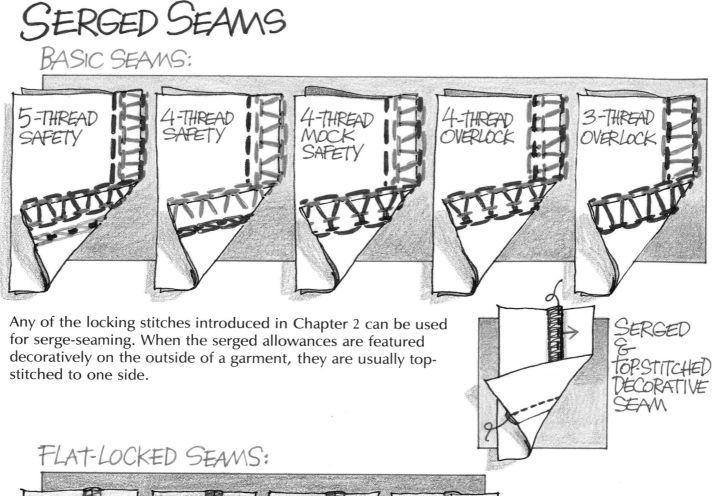

5-THREAD SAFETY

4-THREAD SAFETY

4-THREAD MOCK SAFETY

4-THREAD OVERLOCK

3-THREAD OVERLOCK

Any of the locking stitches introduced in Chapter 2 can be used for serge-seaming. When the serged allowances are featured decoratively on the outside of a garment, they are usually top-stitched to one side.

SERGED & TOP-STITCHED DECORATIVE SEAM

FLAT-LOCKED SEAMS:

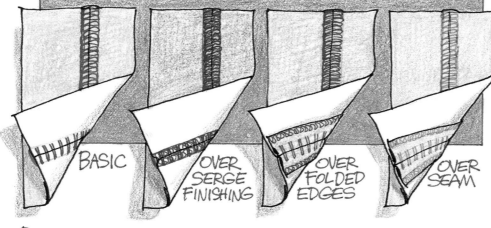

BASIC

OVER SERGE FINISHING

OVER FOLDED EDGES

OVER SEAM

Flatlocked seaming is featured in Chapter 13 for everything from nonbulky lingerie seams to stable decorative detailing. Either the looped or the ladder side of the stitch can be featured on the outside.

ROLLED-EDGE SEAM:

A rolled edge (introduced in Chapter 14) is often used to seam lightweight and sheer fabrics neatly. A French seam (see Chapter 9) is also ideal for sheers or any garment with exposed seam allowances. The fabric is serged, wrapped, then straight-stitched on the seamline.

FRENCH SEAM:

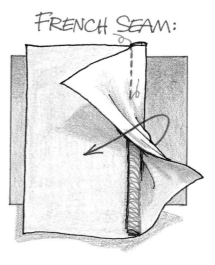

DECORATIVE OR HIDDEN

STRAIGHT-STITCHED SEAMS:

BASIC

TWIN-NEEDLE SEAMING — SERGE ALLOWANCES SEPARATELY FIRST, OR TOGETHER, AFTER SEAMING.

NARROW ALLOWANCES — TOP-STITCH TO ONE SIDE.

Serge-finish seam allowance edges, then straight-stitch on the seamline. Seam with a narrow zigzag or twin-needle for stretchability. For narrower allowances, straight-stitch, serge the allowances together, and top-stitch them to one side. See Chapter 9 for details.

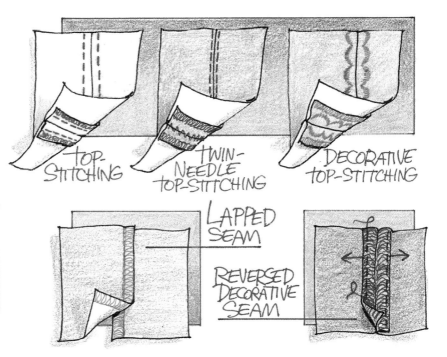

TOP-STITCHING

TWIN-NEEDLE TOP-STITCHING

DECORATIVE TOP-STITCHING

LAPPED SEAM

REVERSED DECORATIVE SEAM

FLAT-FELLED SEAM:

Straight-stitch a flat-felled seam, right sides together. Serge-finish the allowances together, press to one side, and top-stitch next to the seamline and again ¼" away. To reduce bulk (see Chapter 9), trim the under allowance to a scant ¼" and serge-finish the other. Press and top-stitch.

A lapped seam (introduced in Chapter 9) is ideal for reversibles. Serge-finish both seam edges with the needle on the seamline. Overlap the edges, matching the needlelines, and straight-stitch through both layers. A reversed decorative seam (see Chapter 12) is also serge-finished along both seam edges. Then it is straight-stitched, wrong sides together, pressed open, and top-stitched in place along the sides.

Hemming Options:

Serged & Turned:

HEM ALLOWANCE

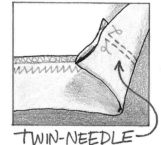

TWIN-NEEDLE

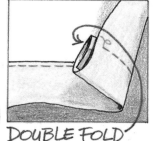

DOUBLE FOLD

Serge-finish the hem edge, turn the hem allowance to the wrong side, and top-stitch it in place using a straight-stitch, twin-needle, or zigzag (see Chapter 15). On sheer fabrics, turn twice before top-stitching. For a hidden hem, hand blind-stitch instead of top-stitching. Or use fusible thread in the lower looper when serge-finishing, and fuse the hem in place.

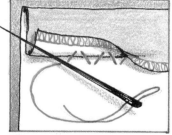

BLIND-STITCH

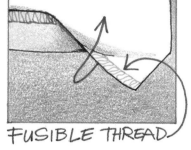

FUSIBLE THREAD

Reversed:

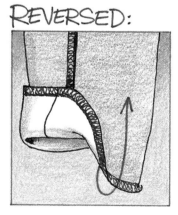

Serge-A-Fold:

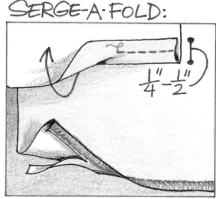

Feature a reversed hem on the right side by serge-finishing from the wrong side, folding to the right side, and top-stitching, blind-stitching, or fusing as explained above.

As featured in Chapter 12, press the edge to the wrong side and stitch about ⅛" from the fold. Using decorative thread, serge over the fold from the right side. Trim away the excess fabric on the reverse side.

EDGE-FINISHES:

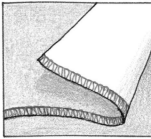

NARROW BALANCED:

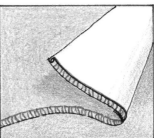

ROLLED EDGE:

Use a narrow balanced stitch (Chapter 9) or a rolled edge (Chapter 14) to hem lightweight or sheer fabric edges. The thread can be matching or can provide a decorative accent. Woolly nylon thread fills in well between stitches for an attractive finish.

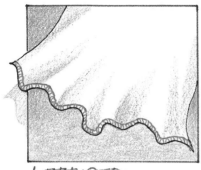

LETTUCED:

FISHLINE RUFFLES:

Lettuce or ruffle stretchy knit or bias edges. Stretch while serging a narrow rolled edge to create lettucing. Or serge a narrow rolled edge over fishline and stretch *after* serging. How-tos are in Chapter 14.

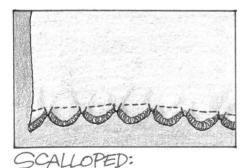

SCALLOPED:

Finish the edge with either a rolled edge or a narrow balanced stitch. Then blind-stitch the edge using a sewing machine. See instructions in Chapter 12.

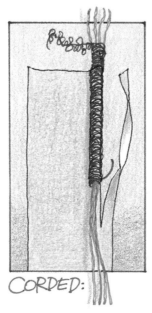

CORDED:

Serge-cord an edge by stitching over one or more strands of filler cord, using decorative thread in the upper looper and a satin-length stitch. Learn how in Chapter 12. Or see Chapter 14 to serge-cord using a rolled edge.

EASY SERGED BINDING

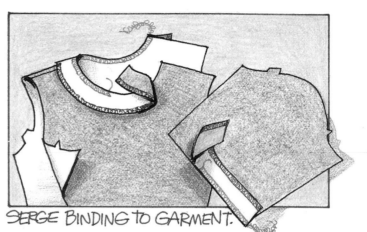

CUTAWAY PATTERN ALLOWANCES.

For serged binding (see Chapter 15), trim off the pattern allowances to the seamline or hemline. Cut a 1"-wide binding strip of bias woven or crossgrain knit fabric the length of the edge to be bound. Serge-finish one long edge. Serge-seam the strip to the neckline or hem edge using a ¼"-wide, balanced stitch.

SERGE BINDING TO GARMENT.

Press the seam allowance toward the binding. Serge the shoulder or underarm seam. Wrap the binding firmly around the serged allowances and stitch-in-the-ditch from the right side to secure.

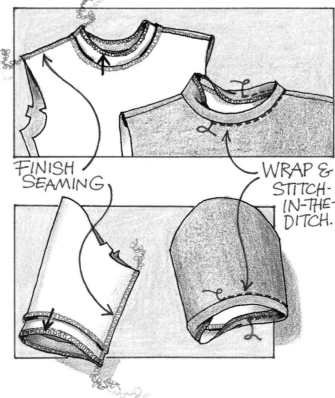

FINISH SEAMING

WRAP & STITCH-IN-THE-DITCH.

8

Handy Control Features

⚔ **Differential Feed**
⚔ **Presser-foot Pressure Regulator**

Differential Feed

Differential feed is an optional feature available on many serger models. If your machine doesn't have differential feed, you can perform similar functions manually (see page 56).

Once you're comfortable using and adjusting the differential feed, you won't know what you did without it. It can be used to prevent puckering on silky or fine fabrics and to prevent stretching on knit or bias-cut fabrics. It can also be used to gather soft, light-weight fabric.

How does it work?

Machines with differential feed have two sets of feed dogs. One set is under the front of the presser foot, and the other set is behind the first set, under the back of the foot. (Fig. 8-1)

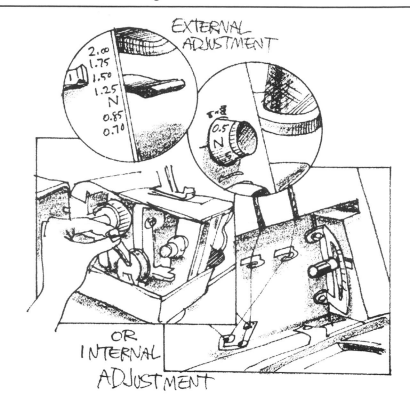

Fig. 8-2: Adjust the differential feed with a knob or lever located on the outside of the machine or inside the cover.

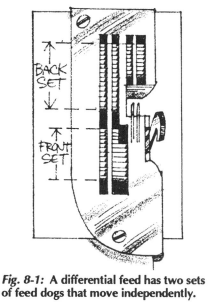

Fig. 8-1: A differential feed has two sets of feed dogs that move independently.

The front set pushes the fabric under the foot while the rear set feeds the fabric out the back. The differential-feed control adjusts the front set separately from the back one. It can be adjusted to make longer or shorter strokes, feeding more or less fabric under the foot than is being fed out the back, so the fabric between the feed dogs is either eased or stretched.

Adjustment guidelines

The differential feed is adjusted by a knob or lever, located either on the outside of the machine or inside the cover. (Fig. 8-2) (Refer to your owner's manual for the exact location and adjustment procedure.) The control can be set at 1.0 or normal (for **equal-feeding**), or adjusted up or down for **ease-** or **taut-feeding.**

Equal-feeding—A 1.0 or normal setting on your differential feed causes both sets of feed dogs to work equally, feeding the fabric evenly without easing or stretching.

Ease-feeding—When the differential feed is set above the 1.0 or normal setting, fabric feeds under the front of the foot faster than it is fed out the back, as if you were pushing more fabric under the foot than it normally takes. The higher the setting, the more easing. (Fig. 8-3) Ease-feeding is ideal for serging sweater knits, ribbing, bias-cut fabrics, or other loosely constructed fabrics that may stretch when stitched. It eliminates wavy seams and stretched edges.

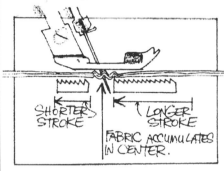

Fig. 8-3: During ease-feeding, fabric is fed into the machine faster than it is fed out.

Taut-feeding—With a differential feed setting less than 1.0 or normal, fabric is fed under the foot more slowly than it is fed out the back, as if you tugged on the fabric to hold it back as it feeds. The lower the setting, the more taut the fabric. (Fig. 8-4)

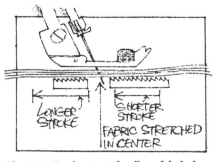

Fig. 8-4: During taut-feeding, fabric is fed into the machine more slowly than it is fed out.

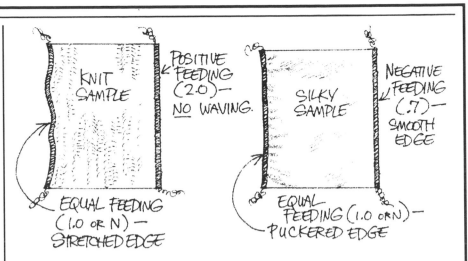

Fig. 8-5: **Test-serge samples to see the results of the differential feed.**

Because the fabric is stretched taut between the sets of feed dogs, any puckering is eliminated. Taut-feeding is most often used for serging lightweight silky or sheer fabrics that normally might pucker when stitched.

Practice using the differential feed by serging one side of a knit sample using the 1.0 or normal setting (equal-feeding). Then adjust to a 2.0 (ease-feeding) setting and serge the other side of the sample. (Fig. 8-5) Repeat the exercise using silky fabric and 1.0 or normal (equal-feeding) and .7 or .5 (taut-feeding) settings.

Differential-feed gathering

Use the differential feed to gather a single layer of soft, lightweight fabric. This technique works well for easing in a sleeve cap or for quick gathering and ruffling when precision isn't vital. Softer fabric, such as tricot or interlock, will gather more than stiff fabric.

1. Begin with a medium (or normal) stitch length and the highest differential-feed setting (2.0).

2. Serge the fabric edge, allowing the fabric to feed freely into the machine. (Fig. 8-6)

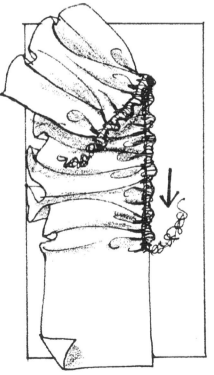

Fig. 8-6: **To gather with the differential feed, use a medium to long stitch and a 2.0 differential feed setting.**

3. Lengthen the stitch for more gathering. For fewer gathers, decrease the stitch length or the differential-feed setting.

> *For even more gathering, tighten the needle-thread tension.*
> **Naomi Baker**
>
> *Differential-feed gathering is perfect for easing a sleeve cap before setting it into a garment.*
> **Ruthann Spiegelhoff**

If you don't have differential feed

Those who don't have differential feed can avoid puckered or stretched seams by manually manipulating the fabric (or by regulating the presser-foot pressure, which we'll discuss later in this chapter).

Ease-plus—Replicate the differential feed's ease-feeding function by using your right-hand fingertips to gently feed the fabric under the front of the foot faster than the feed dogs would normally take it in. Also hold the fabric against the back of the presser foot with your left index finger, slowing down its exit from under the foot. (Fig. 8-7) Like ease-feeding, ease-plussing will eliminate stretching or waving of sweater knits, ribbing, bias-cut edges, or loosely constructed fabric.

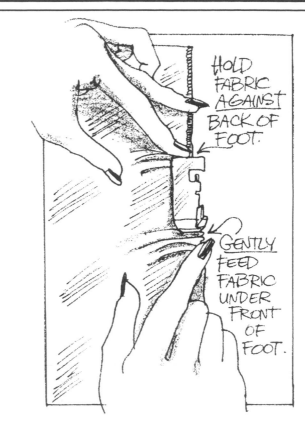

Fig. 8-7: Ease-plus stretchy or loosely woven fabrics manually when a differential feed is not available.

> *Remember, a longer stitch will also eliminate a lot of stretching, and a shorter stitch can help prevent puckering.*
> **Jan Saunders**

Taut serging—As with the differential feed's taut-feeding, you can manually eliminate puckering of lightweight silky or sheer fabrics and help fabric layers feed evenly. While stitching, hold the fabric taut (both layers, if serge-seaming) in front of and behind the presser foot. (Fig. 8-8) (**Do not** pull the fabric through.)

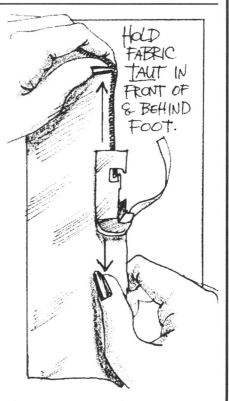

Fig. 8-8: Use taut serging to prevent puckering, but don't pull the fabric through the machine.

Presser-foot Pressure Regulator

A knob on top of the serger (above the presser foot) controls the amount of force applied to the fabric by the presser foot when it's in the down position. The knob will either screw or adjust up and down in stages. (Fig. 8-9) This optional feature can make a substantial difference in the finished look of the edge or seam and is especially useful if you don't have differential feed.

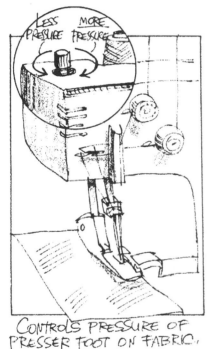

CONTROLS PRESSURE OF PRESSER FOOT ON FABRIC.

Fig. 8-9: A presser-foot pressure regulator is available on some serger models.

When the pressure is increased (or tightened), the foot pushes down harder on the fabric. This is ideal to keep lightweight or silky fabrics from slipping. More pressure on thicker fabrics or knits is not advantageous, though, because the foot will push down and flatten (or stretch) the fabric. When the flattened edge is stitched, it permanently loses its shape. Instead, reduce (or loosen) the pressure for knits or thicker, spongy fabrics. To reduce the pressure as much as possible, on some serger models you can turn the pressure control counterclockwise until the knob comes off. Put the knob back on and turn it one full circle to the right. This is the minimum pressure setting, ideal for serging sweater knits.

Gale Grigg Hazen

Adjustment guidelines

✂ To increase the presser-foot pressure with a screw-type knob, turn it clockwise. To reduce the pressure, turn it counterclockwise. Remember the jingle: "righty-tighty, lefty-loosey."

✂ Increase the pressure when serging lightweight, slippery, or silky fabrics.

With differential feed, I rarely adjust the presser-foot pressure unless I'm serging polar fleece, bulky sweater knits, or other heavy fabric.

Naomi Baker

✂ Reduce the pressure for knits or soft, spongy fabrics.

9

Important Seaming Fundamentals

✂ **Preparing the Seam**
✂ **Basic Seaming**
✂ **Specialty Seaming**
✂ **Securing Ends of Stitching**
✂ **Removing Serged Stitches**

Preparing the Seam

Unlike a sewing machine, a serger trims the fabric as it stitches. This leaves little room for repair once the garment or project has been serge-seamed. To prevent mishaps, you need to do some preparation.

Fitting

If you are constructing a garment, fitting the pattern before cutting out is essential. If you're not sure of the fit even after measuring, cut wider, 1" seam allowances and pin-fit or machine-baste the garment together before permanently serge-seaming. You'll learn more about fitting in Chapter 15 when we discuss basic garment construction.

Pinning

It isn't always necessary to pin the fabric together before serge-seaming, because the serger will feed two layers through evenly. However, if you are more comfortable using a few pins, if your fabric is slippery, or if you're serging something more complicated than a simple, straight seam, you may want to use a few pins.

Be very careful when using pins while serging. Serging over a pin can damage one or both knives and may even throw your machine out of alignment, requiring professional repair. If you use pins:

✂ Position them parallel to and about 1/2" inside the stitching line. (Fig. 9-1) Test your garment fabric first to be sure they won't leave visible holes.

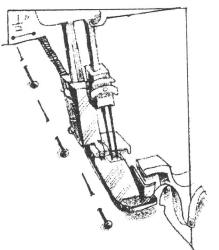

Fig. 9-1: Position pins to avoid the serger knives.

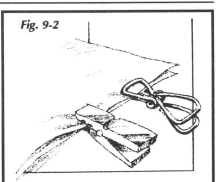

Fig. 9-2

Because serging over pins can severely damage cutting blades, I recommend lightweight, plastic clothespins or clips to hold fabric together when serging. It is almost impossible to serge over them accidentally. (Fig. 9-2)
Gale Grigg Hazen

✂ If you feel you must use pins on the stitching line for a tricky area of stitching (such as a pleat or a tuck), use pins with large, colored heads so they'll be easily visible. **Concentrate** as you serge, making sure you remove each pin before it reaches the presser foot and the knives.

Basting

If you choose not to pin but still want to hold the fabric layers together while serge-seaming, basting is another alternative. Besides machine- and hand-basting, you can use tape or glue.

Basic Seaming

Guiding the fabric

You'll probably most often guide your fabric so the raw edge lines up with the seam allowance marking on your serger (see page 38). For example, if you've cut the garment with a 5/8" seam allowance, the raw edge will line up with a mark that is 5/8" from the seamline needle. This will ensure that the right amount of fabric is trimmed and the needleline is in the desired place.

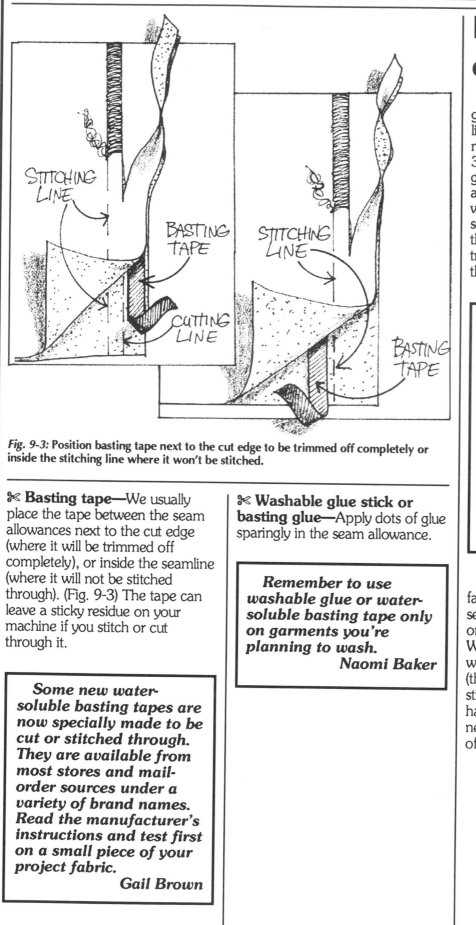

STITCHING LINE

BASTING TAPE

STITCHING LINE

CUTTING LINE

BASTING TAPE

Fig. 9-3: Position basting tape next to the cut edge to be trimmed off completely or inside the stitching line where it won't be stitched.

✄ **Basting tape**—We usually place the tape between the seam allowances next to the cut edge (where it will be trimmed off completely), or inside the seamline (where it will not be stitched through). (Fig. 9-3) The tape can leave a sticky residue on your machine if you stitch or cut through it.

> *Some new water-soluble basting tapes are now specially made to be cut or stitched through. They are available from most stores and mail-order sources under a variety of brand names. Read the manufacturer's instructions and test first on a small piece of your project fabric.*
> **Gail Brown**

✄ **Washable glue stick or basting glue**—Apply dots of glue sparingly in the seam allowance.

> *Remember to use washable glue or water-soluble basting tape only on garments you're planning to wash.*
> **Naomi Baker**

> *Several pattern companies specializing in knit garments use 1/4" seam allowances (be sure to check your guidesheet). In this case, you can generally position your fabric along the right edge of the needle plate, trimming off nothing or barely skimming the edge.*
> **Gale Grigg Hazen**

Another method of guiding the fabric is to line up the desired seamline with the needleline mark on the presser foot (see Fig. 5-5). When serge-seaming, the point at which the needle enters the fabric (the left needle on a 2-needle stitch) is the seamline. If you haven't already, mark the needleline(s) on the top and front of the presser foot.

If you're not feeding the fabric into the serger straight, you'll need to be careful of the knives. Because the fabric is trimmed before it is stitched, the knives will get to it first. Misguiding could result in too much or not enough fabric being trimmed before stitching.

Serged seams

The serger can professionally trim, seam, and finish all in one step. We usually place the fabric right sides together and serge-seam through both layers, aligning the seamline with the needleline on the presser foot and the raw edge with the seam allowance marking on the serger. Leave a 5" to 6" thread chain at the end of the seam and clip it, leaving about 3" on the serger. Always test a seam on actual project scraps before serge-seaming your garment fabric.

> *For very soft or stretchy fabric such as sweater knits, I recommend stabilizing seams with clear elastic in either the 3/8" or 1/2" width. It can be sewn through without breaking and is very thin and supple. Because it has some give, it doesn't cause rigid or puckered seams.*
> **Gale Grigg Hazen**

Note: Don't trim off the thread chains at the beginning and end of serged seams; they'll keep the fabric from separating until you secure the stitching. (We'll cover securing the stitching later in the chapter.)

3-thread or 4-thread seam (Fig. 9-4)—Both stitches work well for seaming. A 3-thread seam has more stretch than a 4-thread overlock or mock-safety seam, while a 4-thread is more stable than a 3-thread. When serging a 4-thread seam, the left needleline

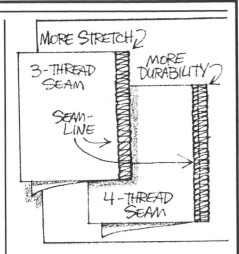

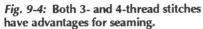

Fig. 9-4: **Both 3- and 4-thread stitches have advantages for seaming.**

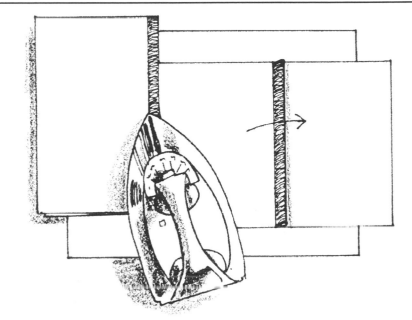

Fig. 9-5: Press the stitching flat, then press the seam open with the allowance to one side.

is the seamline. Use a medium-length, medium- to wide-width, balanced stitch, adjusting the tensions and differential feed as needed for the fabric. Press the serging flat in the position you've stitched it, then press the allowance to one side. (Fig. 9-5)

> *When serge-seaming thick, quilted fabric or heavy wool, first compress the layers with a wide, long zigzag stitch—the left edge of the zigzag should be on the seamline. Then serge over the zigzagging using a wide, balanced stitch.*
> **Gail Brown**

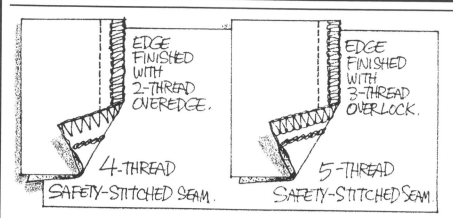

Fig. 9-6: **Both safety stitches are sturdy, with little or no stretch.**

Conventional seams

Straight-stitching and serge-finishing seams takes an additional construction step, but the technique leaves the seam allowances intact for fitting and altering. This seaming method is also suitable for joining heavy or ravelly fabrics that need wider seam allowances.

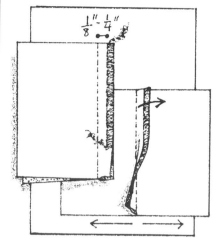

Fig. 9-8: **Straight-stitch the seam. After fitting, serge-finish the allowances together and press them to one side.**

4-thread or 5-thread safety-stitched seam (Fig. 9-6)—These stitches have a chainstitch at the seamline, with the edge finished by a 2-thread overedge (on the 4-thread safety stitch) or a 3-thread overlock (on the 5-thread safety stitch). Both seam types are wide and sturdy with very little stretch. Use a medium-length, balanced stitch, adjusting the tensions and differential feed as needed for the fabric. Press the stitching flat, then press the allowance to one side.

2-thread chainstitched seam (Fig. 9-7)—Although the chainstitch can be used alone for a nonstretch seam, we don't often use it for that purpose. It can be more easily unravelled and is not as sturdy as a sewing machine straight-stitch. (More often we use it as part of a 4- or 5-thread safety stitch or for decorative top-stitching and serge-shirring.) When seaming with a chainstitch, use a medium-length stitch, adjusting the tensions and differential feed as needed for the fabric. Press the stitching flat, then press the seam allowances open. If the allowances will be exposed or are ravelly, serge-finish them before seaming.

Straight-stitched with allowances finished together (Fig. 9-8)—Straight-stitch the seam. After fitting, serge-finish the allowances together with the needleline approximately 1/8" to 1/4" from the straight-stitching. Use a medium-length, medium- to wide-width, balanced, 2- or 3-thread stitch. Press the allowances to one side.

Straight-stitched with allowances finished separately—This seaming method is often used for heavier fabrics so the allowances can be pressed open for a flatter seam. It's not as attractive for seaming sheer fabrics, because the allowances may show through to the right side.

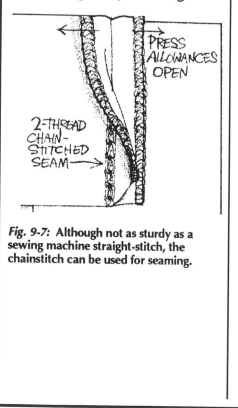

Fig. 9-7: **Although not as sturdy as a sewing machine straight-stitch, the chainstitch can be used for seaming.**

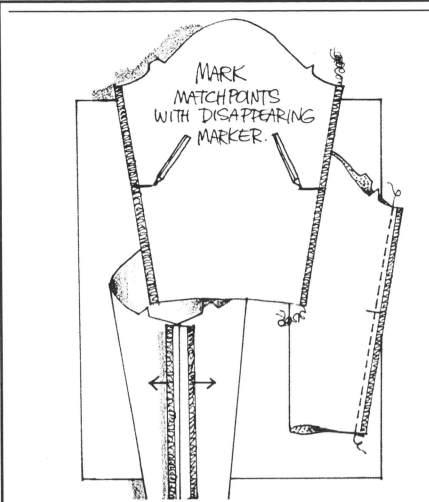

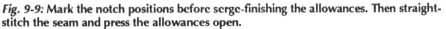

Fig. 9-9: Mark the notch positions before serge-finishing the allowances. Then straight-stitch the seam and press the allowances open.

1. For clean, ravel-free edges, serge-finish the seam allowances as soon as you mark the match-points and remove the pattern tissue. When serging, skim the stray threads only, leaving the original width of the seam allowance intact. Use a medium-length, medium- to wide-width, balanced, 2- or 3-thread stitch. With this method, the edges are much easier to maneuver while being finished and are ravel-free during construction.

2. Place the fabric layers right sides together and straight-stitch the seam. Press the allowances open.

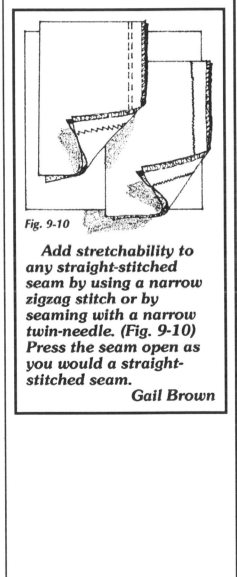

Fig. 9-10

Add stretchability to any straight-stitched seam by using a narrow zigzag stitch or by seaming with a narrow twin-needle. (Fig. 9-10) Press the seam open as you would a straight-stitched seam.
Gail Brown

Note: When using this seaming method, mark the notch positions and matchpoints with a disappearing marker before serge-finishing. The actual notches will be trimmed off before the seam is stitched. (Fig. 9-9)

For accuracy, I draw a line across the allowance with a disappearing marker to mark the notches so I can later locate the exact position. This works the same as a snip notch, which can't be used because it would cut too close to the seamline.
Jan Saunders

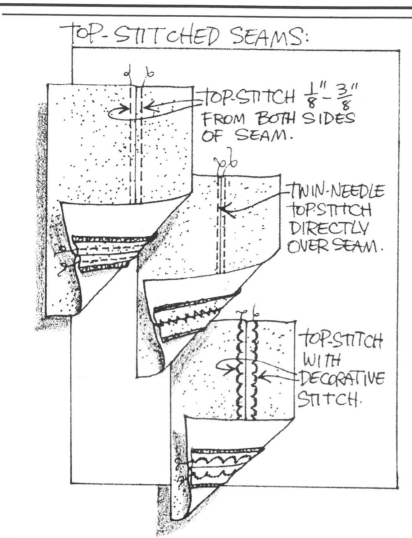

TOP-STITCHED SEAMS:

TOP-STITCH $\frac{1}{8}''$ - $\frac{3}{8}''$ FROM BOTH SIDES OF SEAM.

TWIN-NEEDLE TOP-STITCH DIRECTLY OVER SEAM.

TOP-STITCH WITH DECORATIVE STITCH.

Fig. 9-11: **Top-stitching can be done with a straight-stitch, a twin-needle, or a decorative sewing machine stitch.**

Specialty Seaming

Common serge-seaming variations used on fashionable ready-to-wear are easy to duplicate. Always test first on scraps of project fabric.

Top-stitched seams

Add durability and a decorative touch to the serge-finished and straight-stitched seam described previously.

1. Serge-finish the seam allowances, then straight-stitch the seam, right sides together.

2. Press the allowances open and top-stitch from the right side, using one of the following options:

✄ Top-stitch 1/8" to 3/8" from the seam on both sides. (Fig. 9-11)

✄ Twin-needle top-stitch directly over the seam with the seamline centered between the needles. Use a medium to wide twin-needle (3mm or 4mm). A 6mm twin-needle is also available for use with a machine having a 6mm or wider stitch.

> *For knits, use the new "stretch" twin-needle to eliminate skipped stitches.*
> **Ruthann Spiegelhoff**

✄ Top-stitch both sides with one of your sewing machine's decorative stitches or a zigzag stitch.

Serged flat-felled seams

An excellent choice for denim and other stiff or heavy fabrics, the serged, flat-felled seam provides a neat, durable finish. Use it for jeans and for stylish finishing on tailored shirts, shirtdresses, or sportswear.

1. Allow 5/8" seam allowances when cutting out the garment. Straight-stitch the seam, right sides together.

2. Serge-finish the allowances together, using a wide, medium-length, balanced 3-thread stitch and trimming slightly as you serge. Press the allowances to one side. (Fig. 9-12)

3. From the right side, top-stitch through all layers just next to the seamline and again 1/4" away, as shown.

> ***Top-stitching denim is easier if you use a #14/90 denim or jeans needle. The point is sharp enough to penetrate multiple layers of denim easily, without skipped stitches or needle breakage.***
> ***Jan Saunders***

Reduced-bulk variation—To reduce bulk, trim one allowance to a scant 1/4" after straight-stitching the seam. Serge-finish the other allowance. Press both allowances to one side so the serged allowance is over the trimmed allowance. (Fig. 9-13) Top-stitch as in step 3 above.

Lapped seams

Often used in reversible garments, lapped seams are flat and durable. With decorative serge-finishing on both sides, they give a casual, sporty appearance.

1. Serge-finish both seam allowances, using decorative thread and a wide, short- to medium-length, balanced, 3-thread stitch. Serge with the needle on the seamline, trimming off the excess seam allowance.

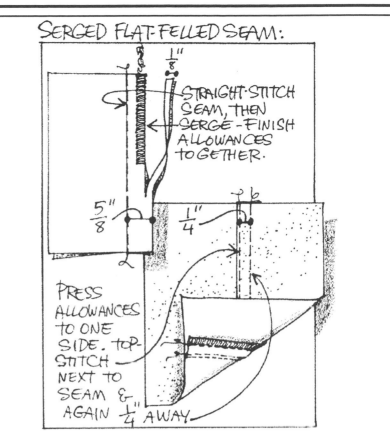

Fig. 9-12: Team the sewing machine and serger for the best flat-felled seam.

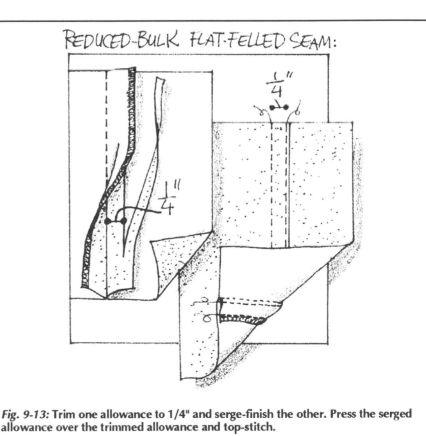

Fig. 9-13: Trim one allowance to 1/4" and serge-finish the other. Press the serged allowance over the trimmed allowance and top-stitch.

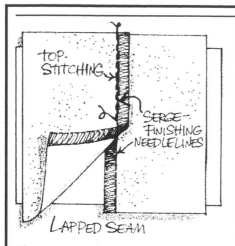

Fig. 9-14: Overlap and top-stitch two serge-finished edges along the matched needlelines.

2. Overlap the edges, matching the needlelines. (Fig. 9-14) Glue-baste or pin in place.

3. Top-stitch along the matched needlelines, through both layers.

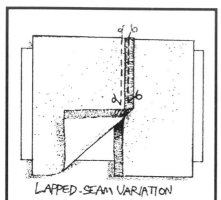

Fig. 9-15

Vary a lapped seam by top-stitching 1/8" inside the serged stitch from both sides of the garment instead of top-stitching along the matched needlelines. (Fig. 9-15)
Sue Green-Baker

French seams

Ideal for sheers or any other garment in which the wrong sides will be exposed, French seams are usually used on light- to medium-weight fabrics.

1. Allow 5/8" seam allowances when cutting out the garment. Serge-seam with **wrong** sides together, using a **narrow**, medium-length, balanced, 3-thread stitch. Trim about 1/4" as you serge, leaving a 1/8" seam allowance and 1/4" for turning, as shown. (Fig. 9-16)

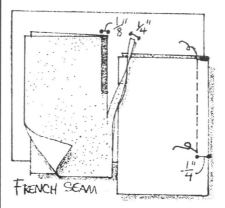

Fig. 9-16: Serge-seam with wrong sides together. Press the fabric right sides together, enclosing the allowance. Straight-stitch 1/4" from the edge.

2. Press the seam flat with the allowances to one side. Press again with the fabric right sides together and the serged seam between them, as shown.

3. Straight-stitch 1/4" from the seam, enclosing the serged allowances. Press the bound seam allowance to one side.

This technique for making French seams takes some testing for an exact 5/8" seam. Use a zipper foot to help guide your stitching close to the enclosed seam allowance.
Sue Green-Baker

Securing Ends of Stitching

Unlike a sewing machine, the serger cannot automatically backstitch over previous stitching to secure it. Often seam ends will be crossed with another seam or row of stitching and will not need additional securing. But when you do need to secure the ends, there are several options.

Seam sealant

This synthetic liquid is clear when dry and prevents threads from fraying or unraveling. Test first for possible staining before using it on a garment or project. Also consider whether the dried sealant will be worn against the skin—it can feel scratchy and irritating.

Seam sealant may take as long as 10 minutes to dry. To speed up the drying process, use a hair dryer.
Ronda Chaney

Use a small drop on the ends of serged stitching. Because a smaller amount will dry faster and neater, use a toothpick or pin to lightly dab the sealant. (Fig. 9-17) When dry, clip off the excess thread chain.

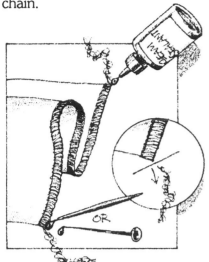

Fig. 9-17: Apply a small drop of seam sealant on the ends of the stitching, or use a toothpick or pin to lightly dab the threads. Clip when dry.

Knot and clip

This method takes at least 3" of thread chain at each end of the serging. Tie a knot in the thread chain close to the fabric, then trim the thread ends. (Fig. 9-19) For additional security, dab a bit of seam sealant on the knot and allow it to dry before clipping the threads.

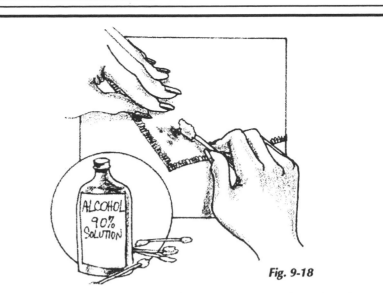

Fig. 9-18

When using seam sealant, keep a small bottle of rubbing alcohol close at hand. If you accidentally drip unwanted sealant in a visible spot on your garment or project, you can remove it quickly and easily before it dries. Gently rub the stain with an alcohol-dipped cotton swab. (Fig. 9-18) If the spot has already dried, continue to rub the spot thoroughly until it's removed. The alcohol evaporates quickly and doesn't usually damage fabrics, but some silks or other specialty fabrics may be particularly sensitive; if in doubt, test first.
Naomi Baker

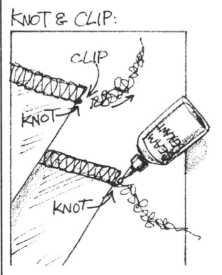

Fig. 9-19: Tie a knot in the thread chain close to the seam. Clip the threads. For added security, dab the knot with seam sealant, let dry, then clip the threads.

Tie the knot in the thread chain loosely around a straight pin to help slide it tightly against the fabric edge. Pull tightly to secure before removing the pin.
Ruthann Spiegelhoff

For a neater and less conspicuous knot, separate the threads in the chain before tying the knot. First, use a pin to pull the needle thread (the shortest one) out of the chain. It's less likely to tangle when pulled. Then the other threads will separate easily.
Jan Saunders

Hook and hide

Hide the thread chain under the stitching. Insert a loop turner, knit picker, latch hook, or crochet hook through the loops of the finished seam, as shown. (Fig. 9-20) Catch the thread chain and pull it back under the stitching. Clip off the excess.

Optional: If you don't have a hook, use a tapestry needle. Smooth out the loops for easier needle threading, then hide the chain under the loops of the finished stitching. Clip the excess thread chain.

Serge over preceding stitches

Of all the securing techniques, this is the most difficult to learn but the fastest to do (once you learn how). It's a bit like backstitching, but instead of actually stitching backward, you'll manipulate the thread chain and fabric in order to serge over previous stitching.

Securing beginning stitches.

1. Begin serging the seam or edge, sewing two stitches into the fabric. Stop stitching and raise the presser foot.

2. Gently stretch the beginning thread chain out behind the foot, smoothing the loops so the chain is thinner. Bring the chain around to the left underneath the front of the presser foot. (Fig. 9-21)

3. Position the chain between the needle and the knives, and lower the presser foot. Slowly stitch over the thread chain for about 1". Move the remaining thread chain to the right to be trimmed by the knives when you continue serging.

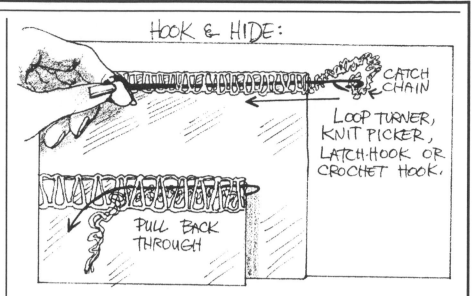

Fig. 9-20: **Run the hook under the stitching. Catch the thread chain and pull it back through. Clip the excess chain.**

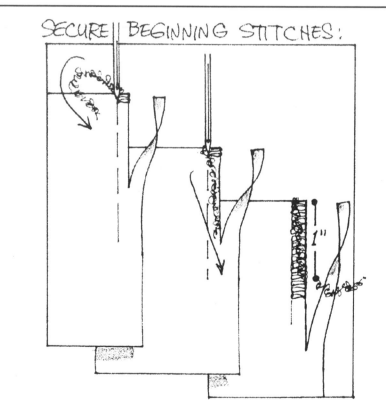

Fig. 9-21: **Serge two stitches in the fabric, then wrap the tail toward the front, under the presser foot. Serge over the chain to secure. Let the knives trim the excess tail after 1".**

TIP: Clearing the Stitch Finger

Clearing the stitch finger is an important but simple procedure used for a variety of serging techniques. Because stitches form around the stitch finger, some always remain there until they are cleared.

1. Raise the presser foot. Turn the handwheel to raise the needle(s) to the highest position.

2. Using your finger, tweezers, or a pin, pull a slight amount of slack in the needle thread just above the eye. (Fig. 9-22)

3. Gently pull the fabric (or thread chain) toward the back of the machine until the stitches slide off the stitch finger.

4. Remove the extra slack from the needle thread by pulling it at the spool or above the tension control until it is taut.

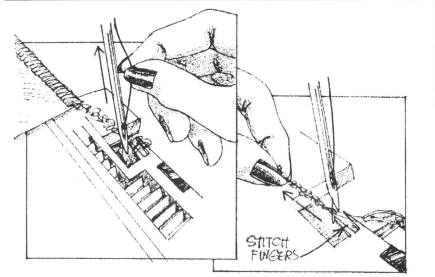

Fig. 9-22: **Raise the presser foot and the needle. Pull the needle thread slack before sliding the stitches off the stitch finger(s).**

Securing ending stitches.

1. Serge the seam until the needle is one stitch off the fabric. Raise the presser foot and clear the stitch finger (see box at left).

> *Never use metal tools such as pins, seam rippers, or awls against the metal parts of your machine. It is easy to scar the surfaces of the stitch finger or looper, causing burrs which lead to skipped stitches or broken threads. Instead, use a bamboo skewer available at your grocery or import store to push against the stitch finger when you can't slide the thread off the back.*
> *Gale Grigg Hazen*

2. Flip the fabric toward the front of the machine and align the seam so the needleline is positioned right in front of the needle, as shown. (Fig. 9-23) Lower the presser foot.

Note: Raise or disengage the knife if your machine has the capability, or be very careful not to cut the previous stitching.

3. Serge over the previous stitches for at least 1", then lift the presser foot and slide the fabric to the left, behind the needle. Chain off and clip the thread chain close to the fabric.

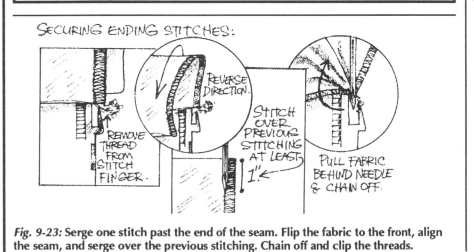

Fig. 9-23: **Serge one stitch past the end of the seam. Flip the fabric to the front, align the seam, and serge over the previous stitching. Chain off and clip the threads.**

Removing Serged Stitches

At some point, we all have to remove serger stitching—to correct a mistake, while fitting, or for an alteration. With the following methods, it's relatively simple.

Serge and trim

Quickly remove a serged edge or seam by serging again, trimming off the previous stitching at the same time. (Fig. 9-24) With this method, your project or garment will become smaller.

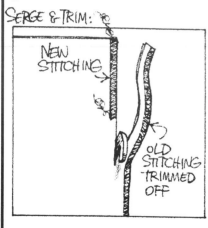

Fig. 9-24: **Remove stitching by serging again.**

Pull the needle thread

The easiest way to remove serged stitches without trimming off the seam allowance is to pull the needle thread(s). On a 2- or 3-thread balanced stitch, you'll pull only one thread. On a 4-thread overlock or mock safety stitch, you'll need to pull both needle threads simultaneously.

> *If the needle thread doesn't pull easily, its tension was probably too tight. Remove the threads using another method, and slightly loosen the needle tension for easier stitch removal in the future.*
> *Ronda Chaney*

1. Clip off the thread chain at one end of the seam. At the other end, run your fingers along the thread chain to smooth out the stitches and locate the shortest thread—the needle thread (two needle threads on a 4-thread stitch).

2. Gently pull the thread away from the looper threads and the fabric. The fabric will gather. Slide the gathers along the needle thread until it pulls out of the stitching. (Fig. 9-25)

3. The looper threads are no longer secured by the needle thread and will pull loose freely.

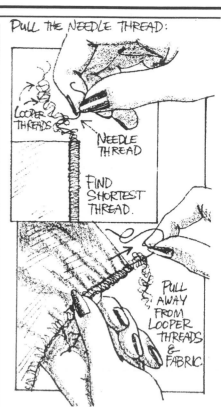

Fig. 9-25: **After clipping off the thread chain at one end, gently pull the needle thread at the opposite end.**

Use a seam ripper

When one looper thread in an overlock or overedge stitch is cut with a seam ripper, as shown, the other thread or threads in the stitching will pull free easily. (Fig. 9-26) The disadvantage of this stitch-removal technique is that many short sections of thread are left and must be picked out.

> *To remove ripped-out stitches, I use an old-fashioned, roller-type lint remover which is wound with wide masking tape. (They're available at discount stores or dry cleaners.) When the tape is covered with threads, I peel it off to reveal a new section, and continue to roll away.*
>
> *Jan Saunders*

Unravel a chainstitch

Whether by itself or as part of a 4- or 5-thread safety stitch, a chainstitch is removed differently than an overlock or overedge stitch. Clip the thread chain just next to the fabric at the end (not the beginning) of the stitching. From the underside, separate the two threads using a pin or seam ripper. Pull the looper thread to unravel the chainstitch. (Fig. 9-27)

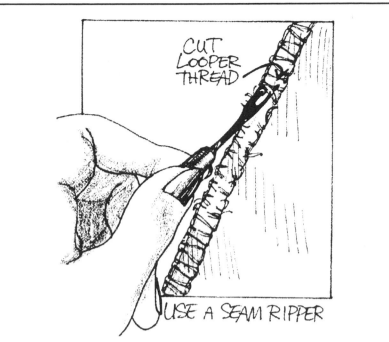

Fig. 9-26: Cut through one looper thread and pick out the remaining threads.

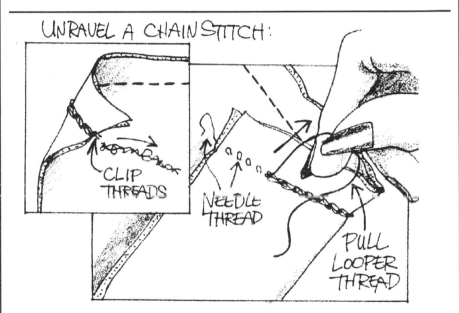

Fig. 9-27: Clip off the thread chain and pull the looper thread to unravel a chainstitch.

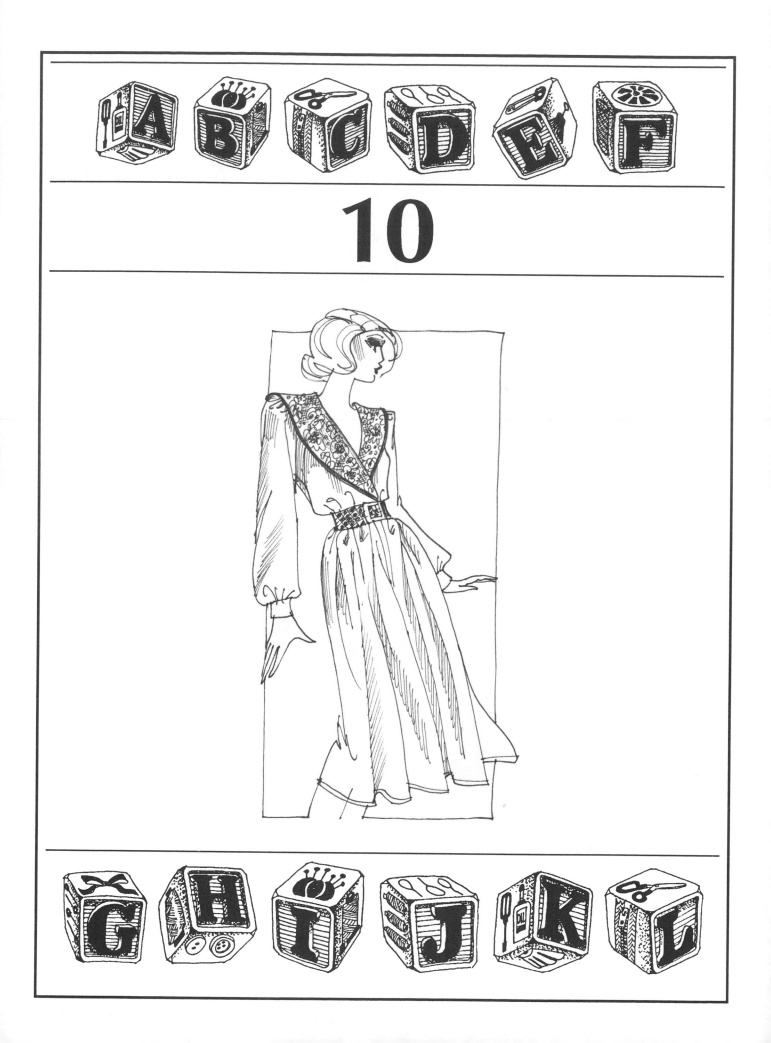

10

Journeying Past Straight Seams and Edges

✂ **Serging Corners and Angles**
✂ **Serging Curves and Circles**
✂ **Hidden Lapped Serging**

Serging Corners and Angles

Accurately maneuvering fabric while serge-finishing or serge-seaming an edge that isn't straight can be difficult, but certainly not impossible. With a little practice, you'll have the techniques down in practically no time.

Outside corners and angles

You'll need to serge outside corners on projects such as scarves, tablecloths, and napkins or the collar points of a garment. Two methods are possible:

Serging off and on a corner—Simply serge off the edge at the corner, pivot the fabric, and serge onto the adjoining edge. (Fig. 10 -1) You can trim the fabric while serging or just skim the edge. Secure the corner thread chain using one of the methods listed on pages 68 – 69.

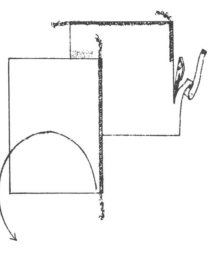

Fig. 10-1: Serge off the edge, pivot the fabric, then serge the adjacent edge.

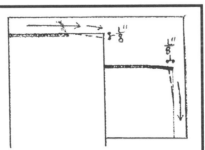

Fig. 10-2

Prevent dog-eared corners by angling in about 1/8" for the last three or four stitches before the corner. On the adjoining edge, begin about 1/8" inside the stitching line and angle out about the same distance. (Fig. 10-2)

Gail Brown

Serging around a corner—
A 3-thread stitch works best for this technique, but you can also use a 4-thread stitch. It looks tricky, but once you master it, you can do it quickly.

1. If you'll be trimming the fabric edge as you serge, pretrim about 2" along the cutting line of the adjacent edge. (Fig. 10-3) This way, you'll know exactly where to turn the corner, and, because the knives are located in front of the needle, they'll need to be positioned right on the cutting line after turning. When serge-finishing without trimming the edge, skip this step.

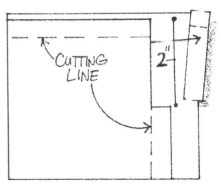

Fig. 10-3: Pretrim the second corner along the cutting line.

2. Serge the first edge, stopping one stitch past the corner with the needle in the up position. (Fig. 10-4)

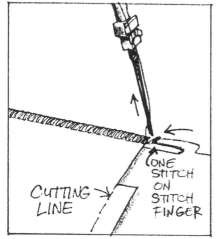

Fig. 10-4: **Stop one stitch past the corner with the needle up. Clear the stitch finger.**

3. Clear the stitch finger by raising the presser foot, pulling a slight amount of slack in the needle thread, and sliding the stitches off the stitch finger (see page 69). Pull the needle thread taut above the tension discs to remove any extra slack.

4. Pivot the fabric, aligning the cut edge with the knife. Lower the needle into the previous stitches on the new stitching line. (Fig. 10-5) Lower the presser foot and serge the second side.

To automatically eliminate any loops at the corner after making the turn and positioning the needle, gently pull up on the looper threads as well as the needle thread above the tension controls.
Ruthann Spiegelhoff

If you prefer continuous serging without taking the time to turn corners, round them off before serging. Use a saucer or bowl as a guide for perfect curves.
Gail Brown

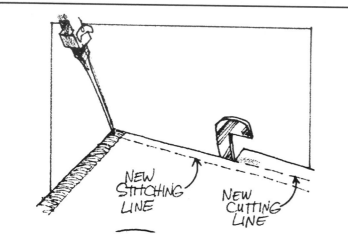

Fig. 10-5: **Pivot the fabric so the cut edge is against the knife. Lower the needle through the previous stitching on the new stitching line.**

Inside corners and angles

Inside corners and angles aren't tricky either, but they may take a little preparation. We use them for slits, square necklines, and appliqué edges.

1. Pretrim the fabric to the cutting line for 2" on both sides of the corner. (Fig. 10-6) When

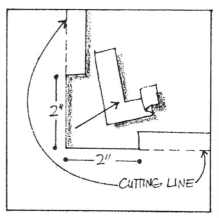

Fig. 10-6: **Pretrim the corner to the cutting line.**

finishing a slit or if the edge is already the desired size, you won't need to pretrim.

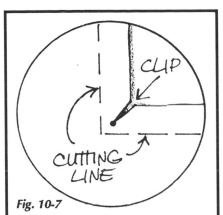

Fig. 10-7

A quick alternative to pretrimming is simply to clip the inside corner to within 1/8" of the cutting line, then continue with step 2, trimming on the cutting line as you serge. (Fig. 10-7)
Ronda Chaney

2. Serge one edge, stopping when the knives are about 1/2" from the corner with the needle in the down position.

3. Raise the presser foot and swing the fabric in front of the foot toward your left, so the corner or angle forms a straight line. (Fig. 10-8) Lower the foot and continue serging.

Note: When the edge is pulled to a straight line, a tuck or tucks will form in the fabric, extending from the corner point. When you bring the edge back to its original angle, the tucks will disappear.

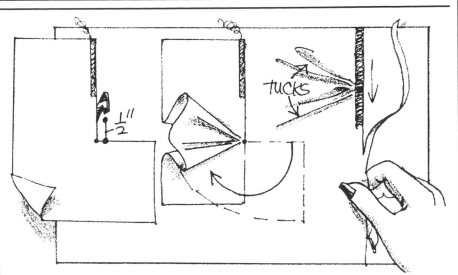

Fig. 10-8: Stop serging when the knives are 1/2" from the corner. Swing the opposite edge to your left to form a straight line. Continue serging, holding the edge straight.

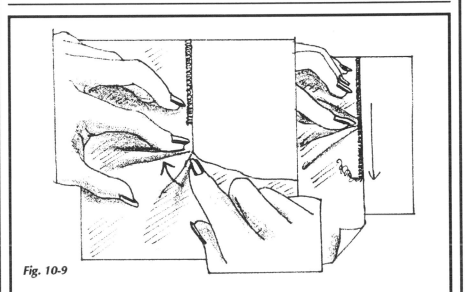

Fig. 10-9

To ensure a perfect inside corner, make several smaller pleats as you straighten the edge. Place your index fingers at a right angle, and fold a small pleat under your left finger. (Fig. 10-9) Repeat several times until the edge is straight, before continuing to serge.
Ruthann Spiegelhoff

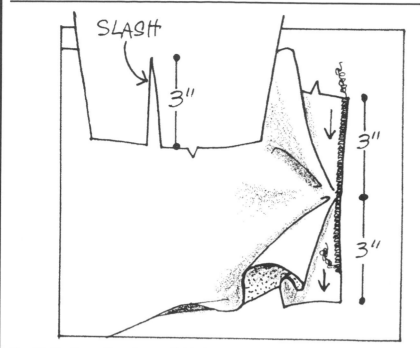

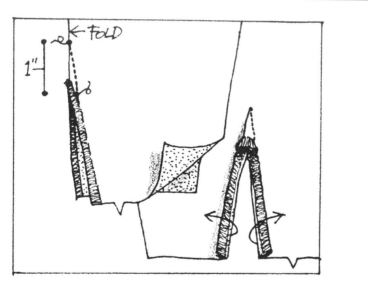

Fig. 10-10: Cut a slit and serge-finish the edges in a straight line.

Fig. 10-11: Fold the opening, right sides together and stitch a 1" dart. Press the serged edges to the wrong side.
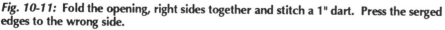

Step 3 takes practice, particularly when you are serging a slit (the most extreme angle). Test the technique until you can do it confidently before using it on your garment.

Serging a sleeve placket

Once you know how to serge-finish a slit, this placket technique is simple.

Note: It's always easier to serge the placket before seaming the sleeve.

1. Mark the placket position and cut a 3" slit. Serge-finish the slit, pulling the edges straight as described previously. (Fig. 10-10) You won't be trimming the fabric as you serge—just guide the slit edge next to the knives.

2. Fold the opening, right sides together, matching the slit edges. Straight-stitch a 1" dart at the end of the slit. (Fig. 10-11) Begin just before the end of the serging, along the inside edge of the stitches, and taper to a point. Knot the threads to secure.

3. Press the serged edges to the wrong side, parallel to the dart edges.

Serging Curves and Circles

Guiding the curve

When serging around a curve, always watch the knives instead of the needle. Serge **slowly** so you can guide the fabric accurately. On an outside curve, gradually move the fabric to the right in front of the presser foot, as shown. (Fig. 10-12) On an inside curve, move the fabric to the left. If a curve is particularly tight, you may have to raise the foot to ease the fabric under it.

> *For more even stitching when serging around curves, use a narrower stitch width.*
> *Naomi Baker*

Serging in a circle

Two methods are used for serging in a circle, where the beginning and ending stitches overlap. The faster of the two is generally for seams and edges that won't show on the right side of a finished garment or project, such as inserting a ribbing circle. The other method, which takes a little more time, is used when the stitching will be visible.

Quick lapped serging—Use this speedy technique for serging a circle where the stitching won't show on the outside, such as an armscye or a turned hem:

1. Serge onto the fabric, angling to the cutting line. (Fig. 10-13)

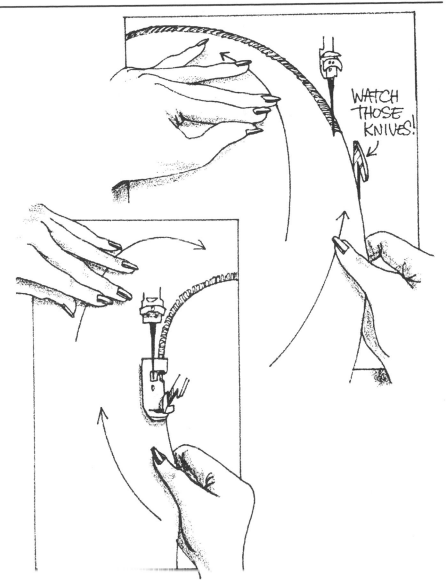

WATCH THOSE KNIVES!

Fig. 10-12: Slowly move an outside curve to the right in front of the foot. Move an inside curve to the left.

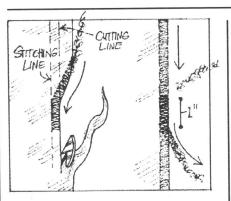

CUTTING LINE

STITCHING LINE

1"

Fig. 10-13: Serge onto the fabric, angling to the cutting line. After serging around the circle, overlap the stitches, then angle off.

2. Continue serging around the circle, overlapping the first stitches for about 1". The original angled serging will be trimmed off. Be careful just to overlap the stitching—don't trim the edge and cut the previous loops.

3. Angle the serging off the edge by gradually moving the fabric in front of the foot to your left. Continue to chain off.

4. Dab the end of the stitching with seam sealant and trim off the thread chain when dry.

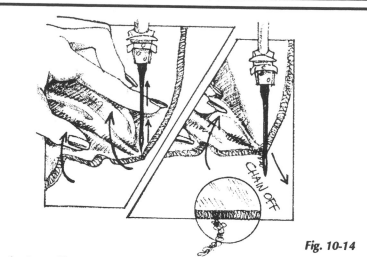

Fig. 10-14

To chain off neatly without putting another stitch in the fabric, raise the presser foot and the needle. (Fig. 10-14) Pull the fabric behind the needle before continuing.

Naomi Baker

4. Raise the presser foot, pull the fabric behind the needle, and chain off (see Fig. 10-14). Hide both thread chains in the stitching on the wrong side of the fabric. (Fig. 10-16) (See the hook and hide method, page 68.)

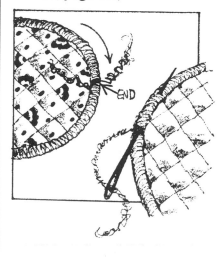

Fig. 10-16: End at the first stitch. Hide the thread tails under the stitches on the wrong side.

Exposed circular edge—

When serging a circle with exposed stitching, such as on a placemat or a decoratively serged neckline, use this technique:

1. If you will be trimming the edge as you serge, pretrim to the cutting line for about 2" where you will begin and end. When serging an oblong or oval shape, it's easier to begin and end on a straighter portion. (Fig. 10-15)

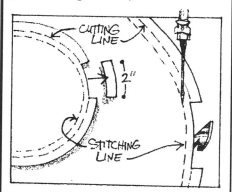

Fig. 10-15: Pretrim along the cutting line for 2". Position the knife against the cutting line and the needle on the stitching line.

2. Raise the needle and presser foot and clear the stitch finger. Insert the fabric with the knife against the cutting line, and lower the needle into the stitching line.

3. Serge around the circle, stopping with the needle right at the beginning stitches in the up position. Be careful not to cut the original thread chain or any of the stitches (disengage your knife if necessary).

I usually overlap the ends of circular stitching, even when it is exposed. Instead of ending right at the beginning of the serging, I take several more stitches, being careful not to cut the threads. Then I chain off as explained (see Fig. 10-14). With some threads (such as woolly nylon) and a short stitch length, the stitching will hold well without additional securing. To secure heavier thread (such as pearl cotton), I often use seam sealant and trim the chain when dry.

Naomi Baker

Hidden Lapped Serging

When using exposed serging on the outside of a project or garment, we sometimes need to close an opening neatly (as when stuffing a pillow) or to correct a section of uneven stitching. To do this, we use a technique similar to exposed circular stitching.

1. Pretrim the edge if it isn't already trimmed. If you are correcting uneven serging, take out the stitches in the imperfect section. Disengage the knife if your serger has that capability; otherwise, be careful not to cut any of the previous stitches when serging.

Note: The serger should be threaded and adjusted exactly as it was for the original serging.

> *If stitches are pulled or puckered, remove them and put a drop of seam sealant on the ends. Clip away the excess threads.*
> *Gale Grigg Hazen*

2. Clear the stitch finger. Position the fabric edge under the presser foot, lowering the needle into the seamline 1/2" before the end of the stitching. Hand-turn the first few stitches for a smooth start. (Fig. 10-17)

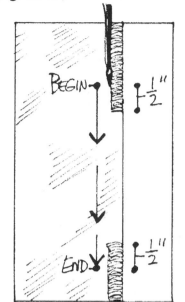

Fig. 10-17: **Begin 1/2" before the open section. Stop 1/2" past it.**

3. Serge the opening closed, overlapping the original stitching 1/2". Guide the fabric so the needlelines match on both layers of serging, but be careful not to cut the threads on the first layer.

> *To join decorative serging invisibly, overlap two stitches. Stop and cut the needle thread about 4" above the needle. Using your tweezers, pull the thread back down to the bottom and through the needle eye. Run the serger forward and off the edge. The stitches will have ended where the thread left the needle, and the loose threads can be anchored on the underside using a needle or knit picker.*
> *Gale Grigg Hazen*

4. Neatly chain off by raising the presser foot and needle, pulling the fabric behind the needle, and continuing to serge. (See Fig. 10-14)

5. Secure the thread chain following the methods outlined previously in step 4 of the instructions for an exposed circular edge.

11

Keying into Special Techniques

⚔ **Serger Gathering**
⚔ **Serger Shirring**
⚔ **Serged Tucks**
⚔ **Lettuced Edges**

In previous chapters, you've learned how to adjust your serger for basic stitching. Now you can use that knowledge (with only minor stitch adjustments) for some of the special techniques that make serging so much fun.

Serger Gathering

You can use your serger to quickly gather an edge or create a ruffle. (Fig. 11-1) A single layer will

Fig. 11-1: You can use several methods to gather with your serger.

gather more easily than multiple layers, and soft, lightweight fabric will gather more than stiff or heavy fabric. The fabric and the type of project will help determine which method you use. Because the seam allowance is limited to the width of your serger stitch, serger gathering may not be advantageous for ravelly fabric or on garments where wider seam allowances are desired.

Differential-feed gathering

On soft, lightweight fabrics, use the differential feed for the quickest gathering (see Chapter 8). The longest stitch and highest differential-feed setting (2.0) will produce the most gathering.

Tension gathering

This method works best for gathering soft, lightweight fabric—a good alternative if you don't have differential feed. It also can be used in combination with differential-feed gathering to increase the amount of gathering.

1. Adjust for the longest and widest, balanced, 3-thread stitch. Tighten the needle tension almost completely. If you are using two needles, tighten both needle tensions.

> *Decrease the presser-foot pressure to increase gathering. You must use strong, high-quality thread for this technique.*
> **Gale Grigg Hazen**

2. Serge the fabric edge, allowing the fabric to feed freely into the machine. (Fig. 11-2)

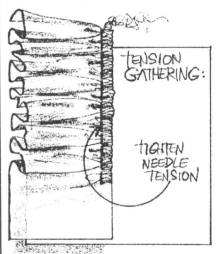

Fig. 11-2: Gather an edge by using a long, wide stitch and tightened needle tension.

3. Test on a scrap of project fabric, adjusting the amount of gathering by varying the stitch length. Use a longer stitch for more gathers and a shorter stitch for fewer gathers.

Needle-thread gathering

Pulling the needle thread after an edge has been serged can also create gathers. Because the needle thread might break when a large section is gathered, this method is best used for quickly gathering or easing a short edge or to add more gathering on an edge already gathered by one of the previous methods. (Fig. 11-4)

NEEDLE-THREAD GATHERING:

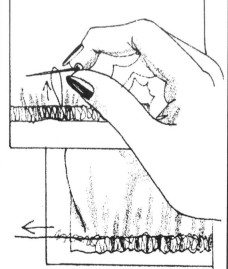

Fig. 11-4: **Pull the needle thread to slightly gather or ease the edge.**

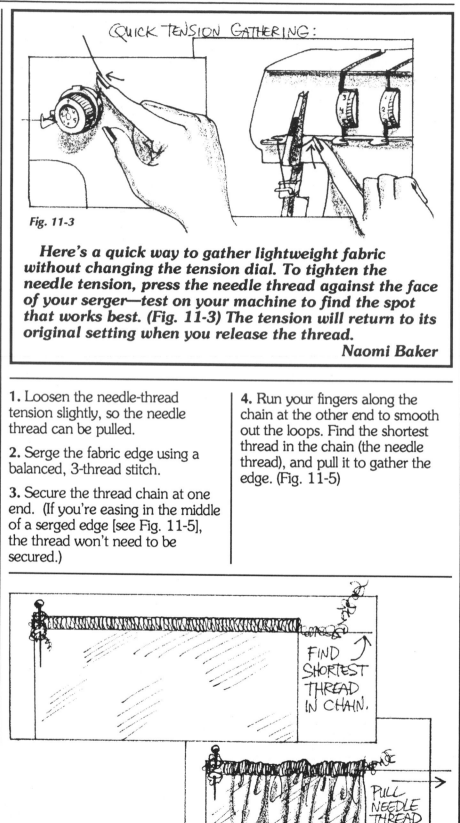

Fig. 11-3

Here's a quick way to gather lightweight fabric without changing the tension dial. To tighten the needle tension, press the needle thread against the face of your serger—test on your machine to find the spot that works best. (Fig. 11-3) The tension will return to its original setting when you release the thread.

Naomi Baker

1. Loosen the needle-thread tension slightly, so the needle thread can be pulled.

2. Serge the fabric edge using a balanced, 3-thread stitch.

3. Secure the thread chain at one end. (If you're easing in the middle of a serged edge [see Fig. 11-5], the thread won't need to be secured.)

4. Run your fingers along the chain at the other end to smooth out the loops. Find the shortest thread in the chain (the needle thread), and pull it to gather the edge. (Fig. 11-5)

Fig. 11-5: **To gather a short section, secure one end of the chain and pull the needle thread at the opposite end.**

Filler-cord gathering

To serge-gather heavier fabrics or for the most evenly distributed serger gathering, serge over a cord and pull it to gather the edge.

Note: When using this gathering method, the serged stitching will lose its ability to stretch with the fabric.

1. Adjust for a wide, medium-length, balanced, 3-thread stitch.

2. Select a filler cord of buttonhole twist, pearl cotton, or crochet thread. Guide the cord carefully over the front and under the back of the presser foot, between the needle and the knives. (Fig. 11-6)

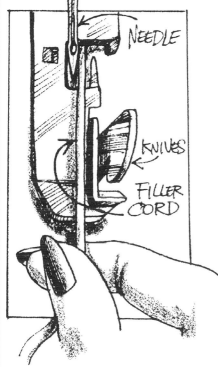

Fig. 11-6: Guide the cord over the front and under the back of the presser foot, between the needle and the knives.

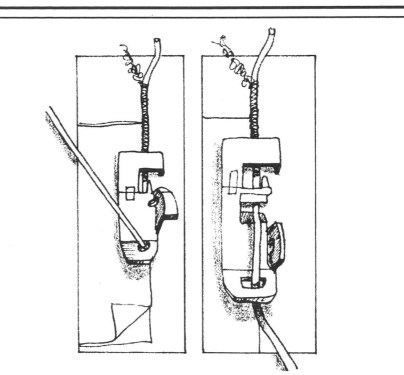

Fig. 11-7: If the foot has a cording or tape guide, use it to position filler cord as you serge over it.

Some sergers have a hole or slot in the front of the foot (called a cording, elastic, or tape guide) to position the cord correctly. If your machine has one, thread the cord through the hole or slot and out under the back of the foot according to the instructions in your owner's manual. (Fig. 11-7)

3. Slowly serge over the filler cord for a few inches, carefully guiding it between the needle and knives without stitching into it or cutting it. Insert the fabric edge under the presser foot and cord, and continue serging.

> ***Build stretch into the gathered edge by using elastic cording as the filler cord.***
> ***Gail Brown***

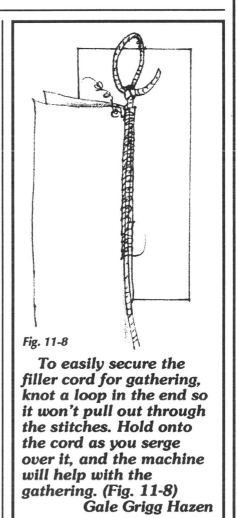

Fig. 11-8

To easily secure the filler cord for gathering, knot a loop in the end so it won't pull out through the stitches. Hold onto the cord as you serge over it, and the machine will help with the gathering. (Fig. 11-8)
Gale Grigg Hazen

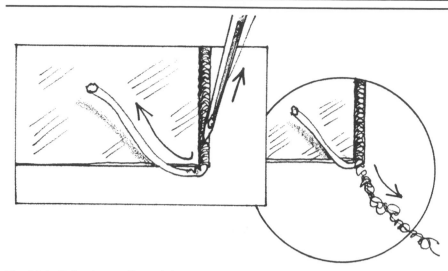

Fig. 11-9: Raise the needle and the presser foot. Pull the filler to the left, behind the needle, and chain off.

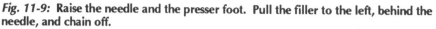

Fig. 11-10: Secure the cord at one end and pull the other end to gather.

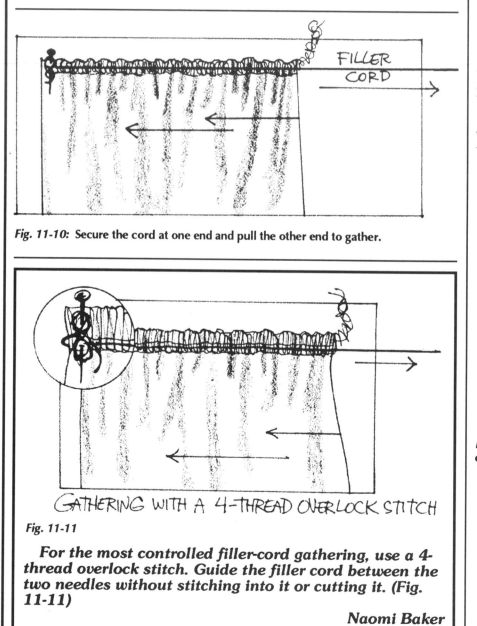

GATHERING WITH A 4-THREAD OVERLOCK STITCH

Fig. 11-11

For the most controlled filler-cord gathering, use a 4-thread overlock stitch. Guide the filler cord between the two needles without stitching into it or cutting it. (Fig. 11-11)

Naomi Baker

4. At the end of the fabric, raise the needle and the presser foot and pull the cord behind the needle. Then chain off. (Fig. 11-9)

5. Secure the cord at one end by wrapping it around a pin or straight-stitching back and forth across it. Pull the other end to gather the edge. (Fig. 11-10)

6. Knot the cord ends to secure the gathering.

Serger Shirring

Serge over elastic cording or clear elastic to create serger shirring. Make several rows for a smocked appearance. Use shirring for a stretchy waistline, cuffs, or neckline. (Fig. 11-12) For accuracy, serge the shirring lines before cutting out the garment or project, because the serged stitches will take up fabric in both directions.

Fig. 11-12: Serge over elastic cord or clear elastic for a smocked effect.

1. Draw the shirring lines on the wrong side of the fabric using a disappearing marker. Space the rows about 3/4" apart.

2. Adjust your serger for a short, medium-width, balanced, 3-thread stitch. If possible, disengage the serger knife (or be very careful not to cut the fabric and elastic as you serge).

3. Fold the fabric, right sides together, along the first shirring line. (Fig. 11-13)

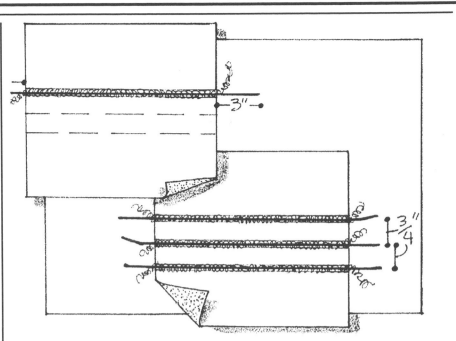

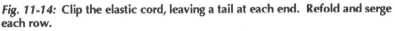

Fig. 11-14: **Clip the elastic cord, leaving a tail at each end. Refold and serge each row.**

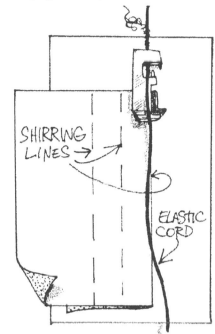

Fig. 11-13: **Fold the fabric along the shirring line. Serge over elastic cord along the fold.**

4. Position elastic cord or heavy elastic thread under the back and over the front of the presser foot, between the needle and the knives, using the same technique as previously outlined for filler-cord gathering (see page 83).

> *Narrow, 1/8"-wide, clear elastic also works well for serger shirring. Use it just as you would elastic cord or thread but adjust for a wide stitch.*
>
> *Ronda Chaney*

5. Serge the fabric fold, stitching over but not into the elastic cord. At the end of the fabric, raise the needle and the presser foot and pull the cord behind the needle before chaining off. Clip the cord, leaving about a 3" tail at each end. (Fig. 11-14) Don't pull up the elastic yet.

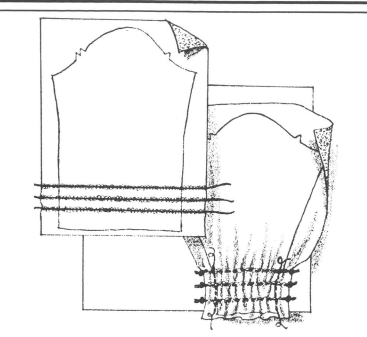

6. Repeat steps 3 through 5 until you have completed each row to be shirred.

7. Mark the outline of your project piece on the shirred fabric. Then pull up the elastic cords the desired amount and knot the ends to secure. (Fig. 11-15)

8. Straight-stitch in the seam allowances to secure the cording before cutting out the piece.

Fig. 11-15: **Mark the project piece on the shirred fabric. Pull up and knot the cords. Stitch in the seam allowance to secure before cutting.**

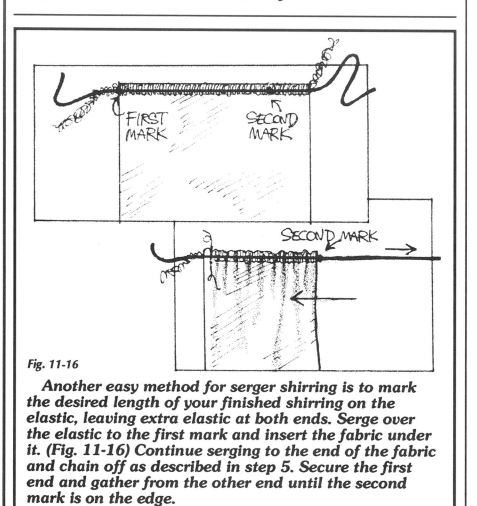

Fig. 11-16

Another easy method for serger shirring is to mark the desired length of your finished shirring on the elastic, leaving extra elastic at both ends. Serge over the elastic to the first mark and insert the fabric under it. (Fig. 11-16) Continue serging to the end of the fabric and chain off as described in step 5. Secure the first end and gather from the other end until the second mark is on the edge.

Naomi Baker

Serged Tucks

Serged tucks down the front of a blouse, around the bottom of a skirt, or anywhere on a garment add a delicate, feminine detail. (Fig. 11-17) Complete the tucks before cutting out the garment.

Fig. 11-17: Serge delicate tucks on your fabric before cutting out the pattern.

> ***Serge tucks only part-way down a bodice to complement a small bust and shoulder area.***
> ***Gale Grigg Hazen***

1. Using matching or complementary thread in the needle and both loopers, adjust for a balanced, 3-thread stitch. On a fabric scrap, test various stitch lengths and widths to see which looks best on your fabric. Because the tuck will equal one stitch width, the wider the stitch, the wider the tuck.

2. Using a disappearing marker, draw a line on the right side of the fabric where you want the first tuck.

3. Fold the fabric wrong sides together along the marked tuck line. If possible, disengage the serger knife; otherwise be extremely careful not to cut the fabric. Serge the fold with the top side of the tuck facing up.

4. Continue folding and serging the tucks, stitching all the tucks in the same direction. For accurate parallel spacing, use the width of the presser foot to guide each new row. (Fig. 11-18) If you want tucks

Fig. 11-18: For parallel spacing, serge the tucks one presser foot width apart.

spaced wider, use the disappearing marker to draw each row before beginning to serge.

5. Press the tucks to one side so the top of the serged stitch is up. Put the pattern over the tucked fabric, placing the tucks where desired before cutting. (Fig. 11-19)

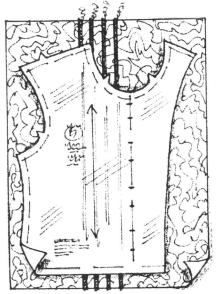

Fig. 11-19: **Position the pattern over the tucked fabric.**

Note: A narrow rolled edge makes a perfect narrow pintuck. You'll learn how to serge a rolled edge in Chapter 14.

Lettuced Edges

On a lettuced edge, the fabric is serge-finished and ruffled at the same time. (Fig. 11-20) This technique can be used only on a stretchy fabric edge, such as ribbing, a crossgrain knit, or a bias-cut woven. It's popular for hems or edges on lingerie, swimwear, and casual garments.

Fig. 11-20: **Create a ruffled edge on stretchy or bias fabric.**

1. Adjust your serger for a short, medium- to narrow-width, balanced, 3-thread stitch.

> *Some fabrics that lettuce best, such as ribbing and interlocks, will run when stretched. To prevent this problem, set your serger as described, but with a very short stitch. Fold and press under a 1/2" hem. Serge over the fold without stretching the fabric. Trim the excess hem allowance carefully up to the stitching. Then stretch the fabric—the lettucing is even and the fabric won't run.*
>
> *Jan Saunders*

2. Use a matching or contrasting thread, and test on actual project fabric before serging the garment. Adjust the stitch length and width to see what looks best on your fabric.

3. Begin by anchoring a few stitches into the fabric. Then hold the thread chain behind the presser foot and the fabric edge in front. Stretch the edge slightly while serging. (Fig. 11-21)

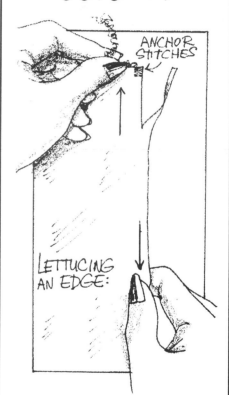

Fig. 11-21: **Begin with a few stitches in the fabric. Stretch while serging.**

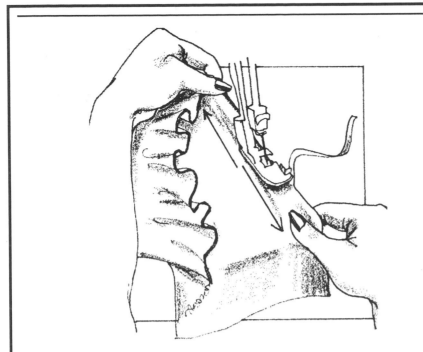

Fig. 11-22: Continue serging and stretching the edge evenly in front of and behind the presser foot.

4. Continue serging, stretching the edge evenly in front of and behind the presser foot. (Fig. 11-22) Be careful not to pull the fabric more in one direction, or you'll bend the needle while stretching. Increase the presser foot pressure for more ruffling. If you have differential feed, adjust it to the lowest setting to add to the stretching.

Note: After you learn the rolled-edge stitch in Chapter 14, you can also use that to lettuce edges. Because the fabric usually narrows as it's stretched, you may have to widen the rolled edge slightly.

On a casual top, lettuce on a fold instead of on an edge. (Fig. 11-23) Using a disappearing marker, draw dots about 3" apart along the lines to be lettuced. Stretch and serge from dot to dot along the folded fabric. If possible, disengage the knife (or be very careful not to cut the fold).

Ruthann Spiegelhoff

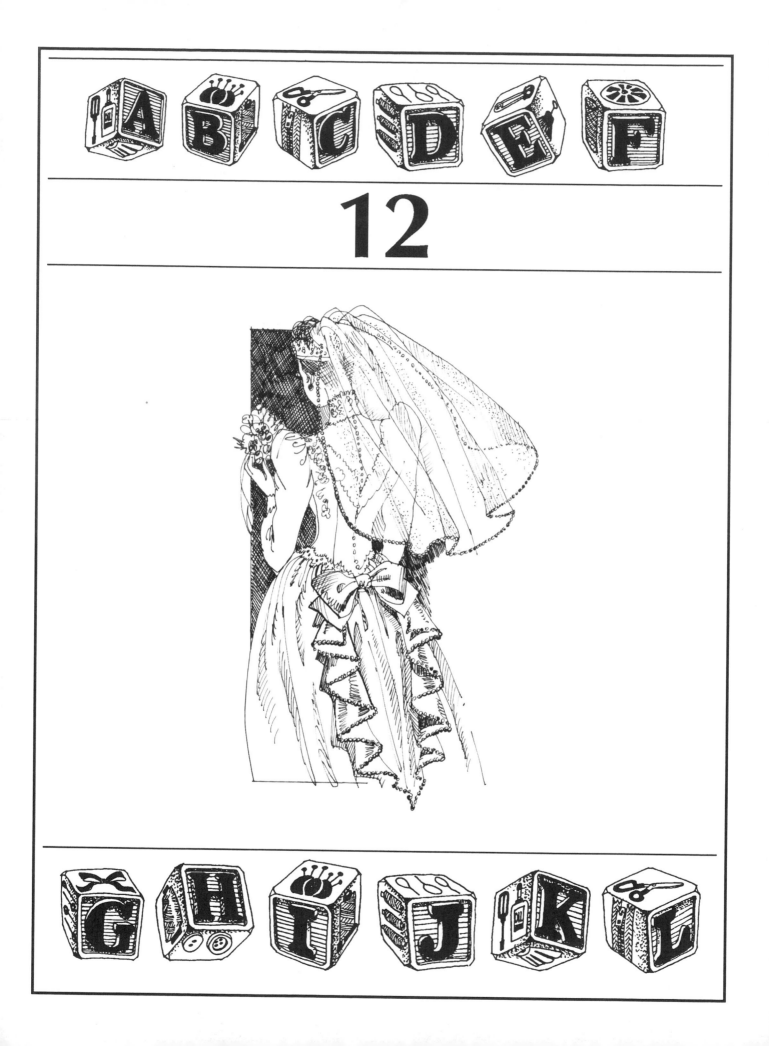

12

Looking at Ornamental Options

- ✂ Decorative Serging Basics
- ✂ Balanced Decorative Serging
- ✂ Constructing Trims
- ✂ Serge-and-Sew Stitching

As you gain serging experience, one of the things you'll enjoy most are the many decorative options. But even a beginner can use basic decorative techniques. This chapter is just an introduction and foundation for all of your future ornamental serging. For more information on decorative techniques, see Other Books by the Authors at the end of this book.

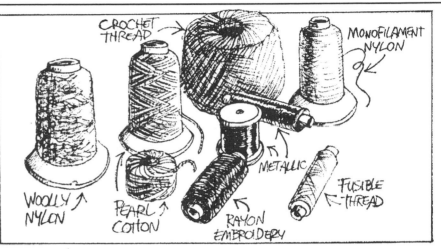

Fig. 12-1: A wide range of decorative thread is available for serging.

Decorative Serging Basics

Threads and threading

Quickly review the information on serger and all-purpose thread, threading techniques, and trouble-shooting tips in Chapter 4. Once you are comfortable using serger thread, decorative serging with specialty threads won't seem difficult.

Several types of decorative thread, in a wide range of colors, are readily available from local stores and through mail-order sources. (Fig. 12-1) (See Reliable Mail-order Sources at the end of this book.)

✂ *Woolly nylon*—A favorite for decorative serging, this crimped, texturized nylon thread fluffs out after serging (with a loosened tension), filling in the spaces between the stitches and covering the fabric underneath. It comes in a wide range of colors (including variegated), is relatively easy to use, and can be threaded through the needle as well as the loopers. Be careful when pressing, because it can melt with a hot iron. You'll usually need little or no tension adjustment when switching to woolly nylon.

> *Make threading woolly nylon easier by putting a drop of seam sealant on your index finger and rolling the tip of the thread for a few moments. This will harden the end and allow it to easily pass through a looper or needle eye.*
> *Gale Grigg Hazen*

✂ *Rayon embroidery thread*—Available in a wide range of colors (including variegated), rayon thread has a shiny luster and silk-like appearance. This thread comes in various weights and is usually quite slippery, needing more tension exerted on it to perfect serger stitching. Lighter weights can be used in the needle as well as the loopers.

> *Always check to be certain rayon thread is securely between the tension discs. For metallic thread, you'll probably need to loosen the tensions.*
> *Naomi Baker*

✂ *Metallic thread*—These threads vary greatly according to manufacturer and fiber content. For serging, avoid those with coarse, metal fibers. Available in a variety of weights and colors, metallic thread adds glitter to serging. It can be used multistrand or combined with other threads. Lighter, softer varieties can be used in the needle as well as the loopers.

> *Don't forget, if there's a notch in the spool, place the spool on the spool pin with the notched end down.*
> **Jan Saunders**
>
> *When using more than one strand of thread at a time through the same looper, make sure both are feeding freely without restriction. Place one on a spool pin and the other on an empty spool pin or behind the machine. Use spool caps or thread nets if necessary.*
> **Gail Brown**

✂ *Pearl cotton*—Now available on serger cones as well as on the original balls, pearl cotton comes in a variety of solids and variegated colors. It is a twisted, 100% cotton thread and has a slight sheen. Pearl cotton weights used for decorative serging are #5 (heavier) and #8 (a little finer). Both weights can be used in the loopers but not the needle. If the #5 doesn't work well on your model, switch to the #8. Because pearl cotton is a heavy thread, you will probably need to loosen the tension on it considerably to perfect serger stitching.

> *Coned pearl cotton does not work well on every serger because it has been slightly stiffened in the winding process. If the thread is not extremely flexible, some sergers will have difficulty forming a loop and won't form stitches. Switch to pearl cotton in a ball if your machine has this problem.*
> **Gale Grigg Hazen**

✂ *Crochet thread*—More tightly twisted but with less sheen than pearl cotton, crochet thread is widely available in cotton or acrylic, in a variety of colors, including variegated and metallic. Crochet thread does not now come on serger cones. Like pearl cotton, it can be used in the loopers but not the needle, and you will need to loosen the tension to perfect the serging.

✂ *Monofilament nylon*—Although not a decorative thread itself, monofilament nylon is used for many decorative techniques. It is a strong, almost invisible thread available in clear or smoke shades. The lighter-weight (size 80) thread can be used in the loopers or the needle. The nylon melts easily, so use a low iron setting.

> *With monofilament nylon thread, you'll usually need a looser tension. Also be sure the thread is engaged between the tension discs.*
> **Naomi Baker**

✂ *Fusible thread*—Used for quick decorative techniques, this thread will form a bond when activated by steam heat, much like fusible interfacing. It is often used in the lower looper to secure edges or position braid. Never allow the iron to touch the fusible thread directly.

Many other threads can be used for decorative serging. Pearl rayon, similar to pearl cotton, was developed specifically for decorative serging. A wide variety of yarns, braided ribbons, and embroidery floss can also be used as well as traditional sewing thread such as buttonhole twist, top-stitching thread, and silk thread.

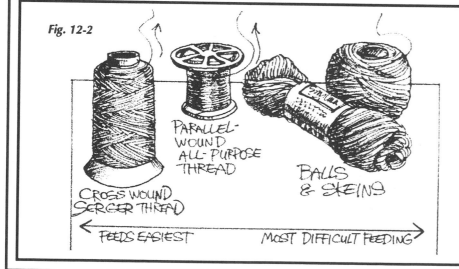

Fig. 12-2

CROSS WOUND SERGER THREAD

PARALLEL-WOUND ALL-PURPOSE THREAD

BALLS & SKEINS

← FEEDS EASIEST   MOST DIFFICULT FEEDING →

Decorative thread on cross-wound, top-feeding serger cones feeds most smoothly. (Fig. 12-2) For parallel-wound thread, such as all-purpose, you'll need to use a spool cap. Anything on balls, skeins, or sold by the yard requires extra care for even feeding.
Gale Grigg Hazen

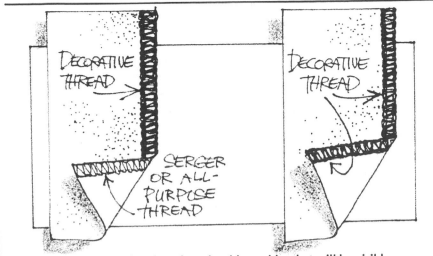

Fig. 12-3: Use decorative thread on the side or sides that will be visible.

Testing decorative threads

Decorative thread is most often used in the upper looper so it will be visible on top of the fabric. When both sides of the serging will show, use decorative thread in the lower looper as well. (Fig. 12-3) **Always check first to determine whether you can use a particular thread in your looper:**

• When folded over double-layer, is it thin enough to pass easily through the looper eye? (Fig. 12-4)

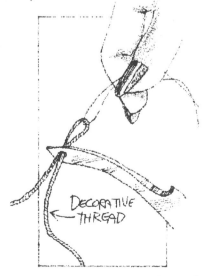

Fig. 12-4: Will the doubled decorative thread pass easily through the looper eye?

• Does it have the flexibility to form a uniform stitch without catching in the loopers?

• Is it strong and smooth enough to feed easily without fraying or snagging?

• Do you have enough continuous yardage to complete your project? For testing, allow at least 7 yards for each looper. (Allow 2 yards for testing if you'll be using the decorative thread in the needle.) To estimate project yardage, allow ten times the finished decorative serging length for each looper.

• If it does work in your looper, are the weight, texture, and care requirements compatible with your fabric?

The ability to use certain decorative threads differs from machine to machine. If a thread does not work well in a looper, you can often serge over it with mono-filament nylon or matching thread. Check to be sure it will fit easily between the knives and the needle and that the upper looper passes over it smoothly.

Follow four simple guidelines to test decorative threads:

1. Allow enough time for patient testing.

2. Serge **slowly.**

3. Change tension settings as you vary the stitch, following the guidelines in Chapter 6.

4. Always test on same-grain project fabric for the most accurate results.

Perfecting the stitch

Rethread your serger with decorative thread in the upper looper or both loopers, depending on where it will be visible on your garment or project (see Fig. 12-3). Then be sure a chain is forming correctly. If not, refer to Threading Troubleshooting in Chapter 4.

As on your sewing machine, change the size of your needle to accommodate the thread being fed through the needle and the fabric being used. No matter what type of needle your manufacturer recommends for your model, you'll find it available in sizes 70 and 90. Use a finer needle (size 70) for delicate fabrics and fine thread. Use a larger needle (size 90) for heavier fabrics and thread, and also for thread such as rough metallic, which provides more resistance. A size 80 needle for medium-weight, all-purpose serging can be used in some models.

> *On some machines you can use a larger 100 or 110 needle. To check, unthread the machine, put in the needle size you wish to try, and turn the handwheel by hand. Check to see if the needle is touching a looper. If it touches, take it out. The value of a large needle is reduced breakage on rough or uneven thread.*
> *Gale Grigg Hazen*

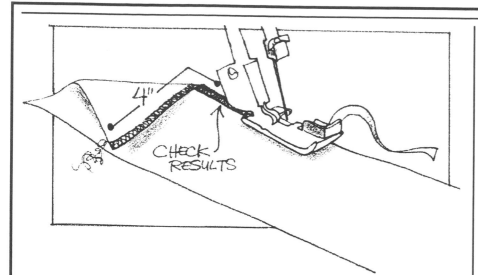

Fig. 12-5: Test decorative serging on long fabric strips so you can check the results, adjust, and continue without serging on and off.

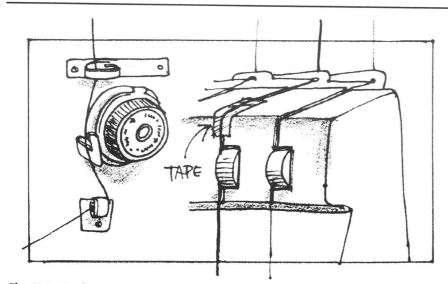

Fig. 12-6: For looser tension, remove the thread from between the tension discs. Place tape over the slot of an inset disc to keep the thread out.

Always test your stitching before beginning to serge on an actual project. For most accurate testing, use long test swatches of the same fabric with the same grain and the same number of layers. (Fig. 12-5) Begin with about 4" of serging, check the results behind the presser foot (without even raising it), and make one adjustment. Serge another 4", then check and make one more adjustment. Repeat this procedure until the stitch is perfected.

Other considerations in perfecting decorative serging

✄ **Important:** If you change the fabric type or even *one* of the threads, you may have to readjust the tension (see Chapter 6).

When a thread is heavier, has more textural resistance, or is stretchy, it will probably need looser tension. When a thread is finer or more slippery, it will probably need tighter tension.

> *I tell my students to remember "tight for light." They'll need tighter tension for lighter thread and, conversely, looser tension for heavier thread.*
> **Ruthann Spiegelhoff**

✄ When you are using a particularly heavy or rough thread (such as crochet thread or pearl cotton), the tension may still be *too tight* even after you loosen the control as much as possible. If this happens, first be sure the thread is not hanging up on any of the tension guides or the thread stand. Then remove it from the first thread guide to decrease pressure on it. If the tension is still too tight, remove the thread from between the tension discs. (Fig. 12-6) For inset tension discs, place transparent tape over the slot to keep the thread out.

✄ If the tension is *too loose* on the tightest setting (most often with slippery rayon or metallic thread), try wrapping the thread twice around an open thread guide. (Fig. 12-7)

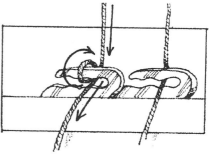

Fig. 12-7: To tighten the tension, wrap the thread twice around an open thread guide.

✄ If both looper threads hang off the fabric edge, even after you have adjusted completely, widen the stitch. This will cause the fabric in the seam allowance to be cut wider, so the looper threads can hug the edge.

✄ Often decorative serging looks best with a "satin" length. This means that the stitch is shortened enough that the threads completely cover the fabric underneath the stitching. (Fig. 12-8) Remem-

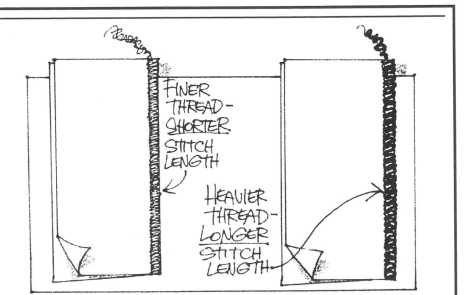

Fig. 12-9: With finer thread, you'll need a shorter stitch length to completely cover the fabric.

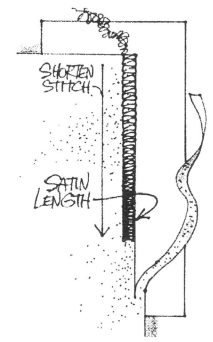

Fig. 12-8: For satin-length serging, shorten the stitch until it completely covers the fabric underneath.

ber, as the stitch is shortened, the tension may need to be adjusted (see Fig. 6-8). The thickness of the thread and the type of fabric will determine how short a stitch you need for satin-length serging. Finer thread requires a shorter stitch for maximum coverage, while heavier thread works best with a slightly longer stitch. (Fig. 12-9)

If you begin serging a heavy decorative thread using too short a stitch length, the fabric can jam under the presser foot. With heavy, decorative thread, always begin testing at a medium-length setting. Decrease the length gradually until the stitches are completely covering the fabric underneath.
Ronda Chaney

✄ For perfectly even decorative serging, your thread must feed uniformly. Be sure to use spool caps, cone holders, and thread nets (see Chapter 3) if they are needed. If your decorative thread or yarn is in a ball, skein, or purchased by the yard, you will need to rewind it onto an empty serger cone or use the "reeling-off method":

1. Place the thread or yarn behind and to the side of the machine. Reel off about two yards, arranging it so that it doesn't cross and won't become tangled. (Fig. 12-10)

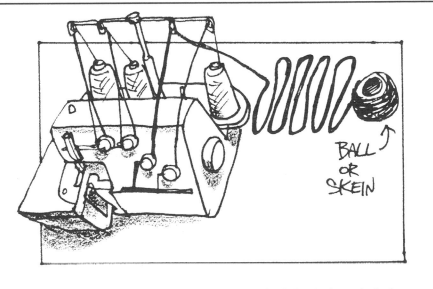

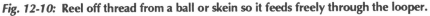

Fig. 12-10: Reel off thread from a ball or skein so it feeds freely through the looper.

2. Watch the thread as you serge. Stop and reel off more thread as you progress.

3. Serge slowly, keeping your eye on the free thread. If the reeled-off thread is completely used and the serger begins feeding directly from the ball or skein, the extra pressure exerted on it will cause a major difference in the thread tension and the stitch will not be uniform.

✂ To maintain an even width decorative edge or seam, always trim a little fabric off the edge as you serge. It is easiest to trim between 1/8" and 3/8", but just skimming the edge to neaten it will have the same effect.

✂ When using decorative thread, hold the thread chain taut as you begin to serge. At times, if the thread is heavy, you may need to continue gently guiding the stitching out from under the back of the foot as you serge. (Fig. 12-11)

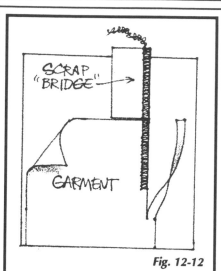

Fig. 12-12

To begin evenly, bridge the beginning of a decorative seam. Stitch on a matching scrap (bridge) and then onto the garment. Trim the scrap tail off later. (Fig. 12-12)
Ruthann Spiegelhoff

✂ **Be careful when pressing.** Many types of decorative thread are sensitive to a hot iron. For best results, use a press cloth to prevent melting the thread or leaving a permanent shine. Treat any decorative thread similarly to a fabric of the same type, and always **test first.**

If you are still having trouble perfecting your decorative serging, refer to the Serger Troubleshooting section on page 139.

Balanced Decorative Serging

Featured in both decorative seams and decorative edges, balanced serging can be adjusted for any width available on your machine. In general, use a wider decorative stitch on a medium- to heavy-weight fabric and a narrower stitch on a lighter-weight fabric. (Fig. 12-13)

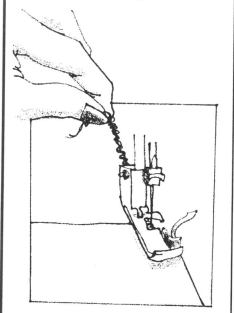

Fig. 12-11: Hold the thread chain taut as you begin to serge with heavy thread.

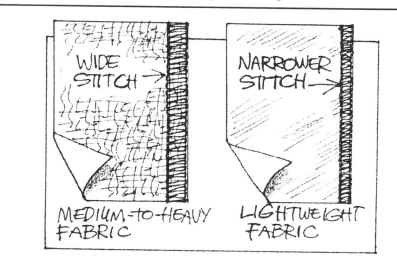

Fig. 12-13: Adjust your serged stitch width to suit the fabric.

The 3-thread overlock is used most often for balanced decorative serging, but the 4-thread overlock is sometimes used as well (see page 9).

Seams-out serging

Decorative seams are usually serged "seams-out," with the wrong sides of the fabric together so the seam allowances show on the outside of the garment. The needleline (left needleline on a 4-thread) is still the seamline, but the serged allowances become a decorative element on the right side. (Fig. 12-14)

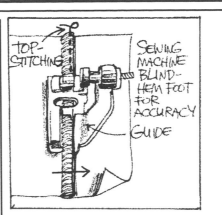

Fig. 12-15: **Top-stitch the serged allowances to one side for durability and neatness.**

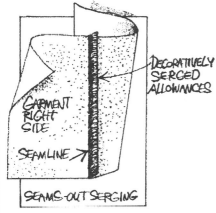

Fig. 12-14: **When the seam is serged with wrong sides together, the allowances are featured on the right side.**

The serged-together allowances, especially wide ones, are often top-stitched to one side for neatness and durability. For most accuracy, use a blindhem foot on your sewing machine to guide the top-stitching evenly along the overlocked edge. (Fig. 12-15)

> *If you'll be top-stitching the seam to one side, you'll need decorative thread in the upper looper only. If you won't be top-stitching, use it in both loopers.*
> *Sue Green-Baker*

Reversed decorative seams

Another way to feature decoratively serge-finished seam allowances on the outside of a garment is to finish the allowances separately from the wrong side and then straight-stitch along the seamline with the fabric wrong sides together. When the allowances are pressed open, the decorative stitching is positioned on the outside of the garment. This method produces decorative seams twice as wide as in seams-out serging. (Fig. 12-16)

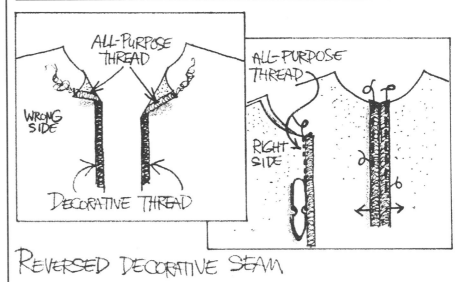

Fig. 12-16: **Serge-finish the allowances from the wrong side, straight-stitch the seam, then press it open and top-stitch.**

1. Adjust your serger for a wide, satin-length, balanced, 3-thread stitch. Use decorative thread in the upper looper and matching serger or all-purpose thread in the needle and lower looper.

2. Serge-finish the seam allowances from the **wrong** side, positioning the needleline on the seamline and trimming the excess allowance.

> *If the fabric has a tendency to stretch while you are serge-finishing, adjust your differential feed to a setting greater than 1.0, ease-plus manually (see Fig. 8-7), or lengthen the stitch slightly.*
> *Naomi Baker*

3. Place the fabric wrong sides together. Using an adjustable zipper foot, straight-stitch the two pieces together along the needlelines of the decorative stitching. It will help to pin at regular intervals and stitch slowly.

4. Using a press cloth, steam the seam allowances open on the right side of the fabric. Then top-stitch them down along both outside edges.

> *Use fusible thread in the lower looper of the decorative serging when constructing reversed decorative seams. When you steam the allowances open, you can fuse them into position at the same time.*
> *Naomi Baker*

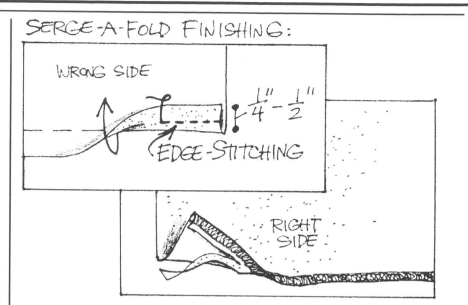

Fig. 12-17: Press the edge to the wrong side and edge-stitch. Serge over the fold from the right side and trim away the excess fabric.

Serge-a-fold finishing

Balanced decorative serging can be used for both seams and edges. On some fabrics, however, the edges will need more body and stability than a single row of serging can provide. Fold the edge before serge-finishing and place the decorative serging over the fold to finish the edge neatly and stabilize it as well. (Fig. 12-17)

1. Press 1/4" to 1/2" to the wrong side of the fabric. The amount you need to turn under will depend on your fabric and the width of your stitch, so test first. You'll need to press under more fabric if the stitch is wide or the fabric is difficult to handle.

2. For easiest handling of difficult fabrics, top-stitch about 1/8" from the fold. If your fabric is stable and holds a crisp fold, this step may not be necessary.

3. Adjust your serger for a satin-length, balanced, 3-thread stitch of any width. Use decorative thread in the upper looper if only the right side will show, or use it in both loopers if both sides will show. Use matching serger or all-purpose thread in the needle.

4. From the right side, serge along the fold, covering the top-stitching without cutting the fabric. (Disengage the knife if possible.)

5. Trim away the excess turned-back fabric from the wrong side.

> *If the edge will be seen from both sides, you may choose to trim the excess fabric next to the top-stitching before serge-finishing the fold, so the serging will completely cover the cut edge.*
> *Gail Brown*

Note: After you learn the rolled edge-stitch in Chapter 14, you can use the serge-a-fold technique to perfect narrow rolled edges, too.

Serge-corded edges

Add stability to an edge and give it an attractive corded finish at the same time by serging over filler cord—one or more strands of crochet thread or other heavy thread or cording. Using heavier filler cord or more strands will increase the corded effect. Because of the filler cord, a serge-corded edge will not stretch with the fabric. (Fig. 12-18)

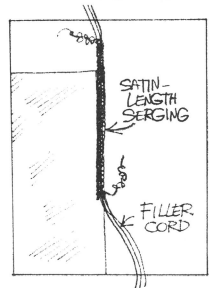

Fig. 12-18: Use filler cord to stabilize an edge and give it a corded finish.

1. Adjust your serger for a satin-length, medium- to narrow-width, balanced, 3-thread stitch. Use decorative thread in the upper looper if only the right side of the fabric will show, or use it in both loopers if both sides will show. Complete the threading with all-purpose or serger thread.

Note: When you learn flatlocking in Chapter 13 and rolled edges in Chapter 14, you can also use those stitches for serging over filler cord.

2. If your serger has a special foot for guiding cording (see Fig. 2-10), use it. Select heavy thread or cord (filler cord) to match your decorative thread.

> *Use elastic cording as filler cord to build stretch into the corded edge. This works well for serge-cording sweatering, interlocks, and other knits.*
> **Naomi Baker**
>
> *Try 1/8" clear elastic for an attractive serge-corded edge. It works nicely on ribbing.*
> **Ruthann Spiegelhoff**

3. Although the stitch is adjusted differently, this technique is similar to filler-cord gathering (page 83). Feed the cording through your special presser foot or guide it over the front and under the back of any standard foot, between the needle and the knives. (Fig. 12-19)

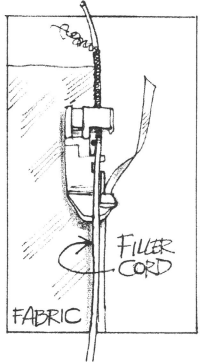

Fig. 12-19: Feed the filler cord over the front and under the back of a standard presser foot, guiding it between the needle and the knives.

4. Turn the handwheel to form a few stitches over the filler cord. Be careful to stitch over the filler, not through it. Then serge slowly for a few inches, testing to be sure the stitches are forming evenly. If the filler is too thick, use a thinner cording or remove one or more strands of the heavy thread until you can serge over it smoothly.

5. Insert the fabric under the presser foot and serge **slowly** for the most consistent stitch formation. Leave several inches of filler extending at the end of the serging.

6. To ease in a curved or stretched edge, pull up on the filler and knot it securely.

> *For a more durable edge, combine the serge-corded edge technique with serge-a-fold finishing (see page 98).*
> **Gail Brown**
>
> *After you gain more experience with serge-corded edges, you can try serging over ribbon, yarn, beads, and sequins. To float a decorative filler on the fabric, use a longer stitch with monofilament nylon in the upper looper. See the Know Your Serger series (listed on page 144) for more advanced instructions.*
> **Naomi Baker**

Constructing Trims

Not only can you decoratively serge directly onto your garment or project, but you can also serge a variety of attractive trims for separate application. By serging trims yourself, you'll save time and money shopping for the right braid or binding, and you'll also have a perfect match.

Serged braid

Basic serged braid is constructed by serge-finishing both long edges of a bias strip with the needlelines on top of each other. (Fig. 12-20)

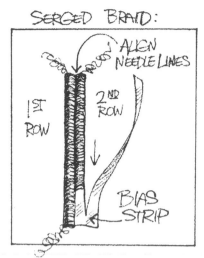

Fig. 12-20: Serge-finish both long edges of a bias strip with the needlelines matching.

> *Serged braids are also soft and often more flexible than purchased varieties, so more intricate designs are much easier to apply.*
> Jan Saunders

1. Adjust your serger for a wide, satin-length, balanced, 3-thread stitch. Use decorative thread in the upper looper and matching all-purpose or serger thread in the needle and lower looper.

2. Cut a bias strip of medium-weight fabric the length you'll want your finished braid plus at least 1/4". To prevent show-through, use a fabric that blends or color-coordinates with the decorative thread.

> *For a quick braid base fabric, use 1/2"-wide, color-coordinated, single-fold bias tape. Press it flat before serge-finishing.*
> Ronda Chaney

3. Serge one long edge with the needleline approximately in the center of the strip. Unless you are serging over a folded edge, you'll be trimming at least 1/8" for accuracy.

4. Reverse the strip and serge-finish the opposite edge, aligning the needlelines. To guide the second needleline directly over the first, use the needleline marking on your presser foot (see page 38).

You can use any type and color of thread, any stitch with or without filler cord, and any base fabric to construct serged braid. Mix colors and textures for unique braids. Leave fabric exposed

between the rows of stitching when you want to feature it as part of the trim. (Fig. 12-21) After you learn flatlocking and rolled edges in the next two chapters, you can use these stitches for braids, too.

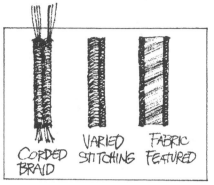

Fig. 12-21: **Create novelty braids by varying the thread or stitch. You can leave fabric exposed as part of the braid.**

Serged binding

The major difference in constructing serged braid and serged binding is that for binding you will finish only one edge of your strip and attach the other unfinished side to the edge you are binding.

In addition to decorating an edge, a binding can also help stabilize it. If you are having trouble keeping an edge from stretching while serge-finishing it (especially common on a bias edge or an unstable knit), decoratively serge-finish a strip and use it to bind the edge instead. (Fig. 12-22)

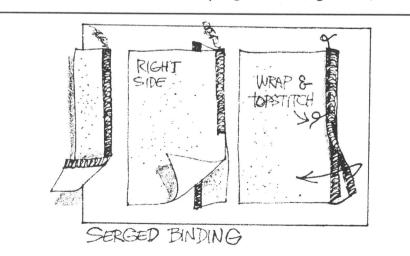

Fig. 12-22: **Serge-finish one long edge of a strip and seam the other edge to the fabric. Wrap and top-stitch the binding in place.**

1. Adjust your serger for a wide, satin-length, balanced, 3-thread stitch. Use decorative thread in the upper looper and matching all-purpose or serger thread in the needle and lower looper.

2. Cut a bias strip of medium-weight fabric the length you'll want your finished binding by three times the seam allowance width, plus a little extra for wrapping the edge. To prevent show-through, use a binding fabric that blends or color-coordinates with the decorative thread, or match the fabric you're binding.

3. Serge-finish one long edge of the binding strip.

> *To be sure only the serged edge of the binding wraps to the right side, measure the exact width of the stitching. In addition to the decorative stitching, you'll need double the stitch width plus a little extra for the turn of the fabric for the seaming and wrapping—assuming you'll use the same stitch width for serge-seaming. Trim off any excess now.*
> **Sue Green-Baker**

4. Place the right side of the binding strip against the wrong side of the fabric, with the raw edges together.

5. Rethread the upper looper with all-purpose or serger thread and adjust for medium-length, balanced, 3-thread stitch the same width as your decorative serging. Serge-seam the binding to the edge.

6. Wrap the binding to the right side and top-stitch it in place.

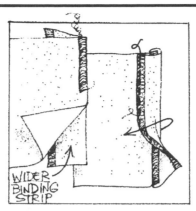

Fig. 12-23

> *For a wider binding where part of the base fabric is featured on the right side as well as the stitching, make the strip a little wider. (Fig. 12-23) Follow the same procedure, leaving extra fabric to wrap to the right side.*
> **Gail Brown**

Serge-and-Sew Stitching

Team up your serger and conventional sewing machine to produce special decorative effects not possible on either machine separately.

Scalloped edging

Stitch over a serge-finished edge with a blindhem stitch to produce a dainty, feminine edge often seen

on lingerie and lightweight ready-to-wear garments. (Fig. 12-24)

Fig. 12-24: After serge-finishing the edge, use a sewing machine blindhem stitch to form scallops.

1. Adjust your serger for a satin-length, balanced, 3-thread stitch of any width. Use decorative thread in both loopers and matching all-purpose or serger thread in the needle.

2. Serge-finish the edge to be scalloped. (After you learn the rolled-edge stitch, you can use it also to serge-finish the edge.)

3. Thread your sewing machine with the decorative serging thread or one that is color-matched. Adjust for a blindhem stitch and test the stitching. For more scalloping, tighten the needle tension. To vary the size of the scallops, adjust the stitch length.

> *With a blindhem stitch, the bulk of the fabric will be fed through your sewing machine to the right of the needle where it's not as easy to maneuver. If you have a shell stitch or a reversed (mirror image) blindhem stitch, use that instead so the bulk is to the left.*
> **Gale Grigg Hazen**

4. Stitch over the needleline of the serging, allowing the zigzag portion of the stitch to hang off the edge and create scallops.

Decorating serged stitching

Highlight any balanced serging (or the flatlocking you'll learn in Chapter 13) with any of the decorative stitches on your conventional sewing machine. (Fig. 12-25)

1. Adjust your serger for a wide, satin-length, balanced, 3-thread stitch. Use a decorative thread in the upper looper and matching all-purpose or serger thread in the lower looper. (Or use decorative thread in the lower looper, too, if the underside will show on your project.)

2. Serge-finish the edge.

3. Put a contrasting decorative thread in the needle of your conventional sewing machine and adjust for any decorative stitch—even a wide zigzag will look good. Test to determine which stitch you prefer over the serging.

Note: You may need to hold the serged thread chain taut behind the presser foot as you begin, so the decorative sewing is guided evenly. Also, for maximum coverage of the decorative sewing thread, you may need to loosen your sewing machine's needle tension.

4. Decoratively sew over the serged edge or add stitches next to it. (Fig. 12-26)

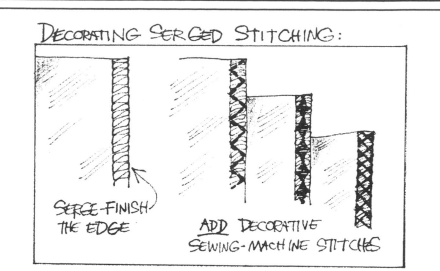

Fig. 12-25: Use decorative sewing machine stitches over a serged edge, featuring a contrasting thread.

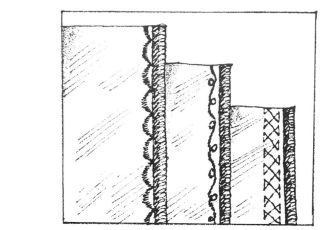

Fig. 12-26: Add sewing machine stitching next to the serging for a different effect.

> *If tunneling occurs when you are stitching over the serging, use tear-away or water-soluble stabilizer to hold the stitching flat.*
> **Jan Saunders**

> *When sewing over the bulk of the serged stitching, switch to your sewing machine's satin-stitch foot (with a groove behind the needle opening on the bottom of the foot) to allow the foot to slide forward easily and not bind on the threads underneath.*
> **Gale Grigg Hazen**

13

THIRTEEN

Manipulating Tensions for Perfect Flatlocking

- Basic Flatlocking
- Decorative Flatlocking

Basic Flatlocking

In order to use your serger to its fullest potential, you will want to learn flatlocking—it's not difficult once you understand the basic principle. First, serge a seam or fold (usually after changing your tensions); then, gently pull apart the two layers until the stitching lies flat. (Fig. 13-1)

Flatlocking is most often used decoratively on the outside of a garment. Another common application is for bulk-free attachment of lace and elastic, a favorite for constructing lingerie.

Adjusting for a flatlock stitch

Because a 3-thread stitch is available on practically every serger model, it is the one most often selected for flatlocking. You can also use a 2-thread overedge stitch or a 4-thread overlock stitch.

3-thread flatlock—Use both looper threads and one needle thread just as you would for a balanced 3-thread stitch (see page 8).

1. First adjust your serger for a wide, short to medium-length, balanced, 3-thread stitch. Thread the needle and both the upper and lower loopers.

Fig. 13-1: **Decoratively flatlock over folds or use the stitch for seaming.**

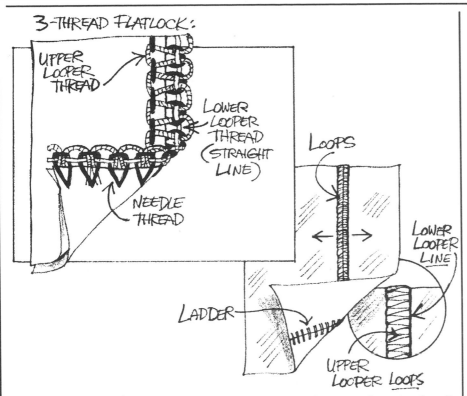

Fig. 13-2: Loosen the needle tension and tighten the lower looper tension. Gently pull the stitching flat.

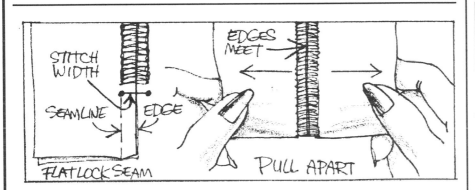

Fig. 13-3: Flatlock with the stitches hanging halfway off the edge.

2. Loosen the needle tension almost completely. Tighten the lower looper tension until the thread forms a straight line on the edge of the fabric. The upper looper usually won't need adjusting. The needle thread should extend in a "V" on the underside of the fabric to interlock with the looper threads at the fabric edge. (Fig. 13-2) Test and adjust the stitch until it looks like the illustration.

3. Using two layers of fabric, flatlock-seam one edge.

Important: When flatlocking, **always** guide the edge under the foot so the stitches hang halfway off the fabric. (Fig. 13-3) You'll have two layers of fabric under the stitching, and they'll both need room to spread out (without bunching) when the stitching is pulled flat.

> *I call this "filling half the stitch."*
> **Jan Saunders**

4. Open the fabric layers and gently pull on both sides of the seam until the stitches lie flat.

2-thread flatlock—This stitch is actually a 2-thread overedge (see page 8) and is available on some sergers (check your owner's manual). If you have a 2-thread overedge, you can use it to flatlock without adjusting your tensions at all. Because a 2-thread seam doesn't lock at the seamline, the stitching will automatically spread and flatten out when you pull it (as in step 4 of the 3-thread flatlock). A 2-thread flatlock is sometimes preferable because it is less bulky, uses less thread, and pulls flatter. (Fig. 13-4)

1. Adjust your serger for a wide, short to medium-length, balanced, 2-thread overedge stitch. Thread the needle and looper following the instructions in your owner's manual.

2. Using two layers of fabric, stitch one long edge with the stitches hanging halfway off. (Fig. 13-3) The needle thread should overlock with the looper thread beyond the fabric edge, forming a "V" on the underside of the fabric. The looper thread should form loops that lie flat on the topside of the fabric. (Fig. 13-4) Examine the stitch and adjust the tensions if necessary.

> *When flatlock-seaming, the fabric is guided away from the knives so the stitching can hang halfway off the edge. The fabric will not be trimmed. You'll need to pretrim so that the allowances are equal to half the stitch width and the needle will be positioned on the seamline.*
> **Sue Green-Baker**
>
> *For easy and accurate guiding, use a blindhem foot (see page 12) to position the fabric while flatlocking.*
> **Gail Brown**

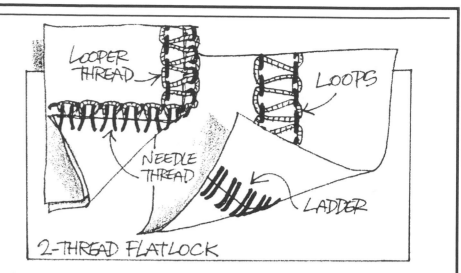

Fig. 13-4: **The needle thread overlocks with the looper thread beyond the fabric edge.**

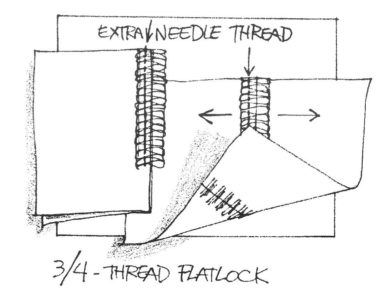

Fig. 13-5: **Seam two layers with a 4-thread overlock stitch and pull flat.**

3. Pull the fabric layers apart on both sides of the seam until the stitch lies flat. If it can't be pulled completely flat, try loosening the needle tension; then try loosening the looper tension slightly.

3/4-thread flatlock—You can also use a 4-thread overlock stitch for flatlocking. Because this stitch has an additional needle thread, the flatlocking will be a little more bulky but is sometimes useful as a decorative option.

1. Adjust your serger for a wide, short to medium-length, balanced, 4-thread overlock stitch (see page 9). Thread both needles and the upper and lower loopers.

2. Set the tensions just as you would for a 3-thread flatlock, except loosen **both** needle tensions almost completely. The lower looper thread will be tightened to form a straight line on the edge of the fabric and the upper looper probably won't need adjusting. Test and adjust to perfect the stitch. (Fig. 13-5)

3. Seam two fabric layers with the stitching hanging halfway off the edge. When you gently pull the stitches flat, you will see two needle threads on the topside instead of one.

4. On some models you cannot loosen the tensions enough to pull the flatlocking completely flat. If so, tighten both needle tensions slightly until a raised fold is formed under the stitching, giving the appearance of corded stitching. (Fig. 13-6)

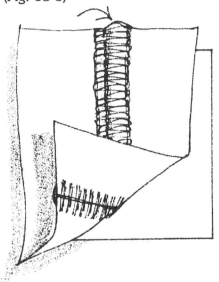

Fig. 13-6: **Optional: Tighten the needle tensions to create a raised fold under the stitching.**

Flatlocked seams

The basic 2-, 3-, and 3/4-thread flatlocked seam is best for knits or other ravel-free fabrics when the seams won't be subjected to high stress. For a flat seam, remember to guide the needleline along the seamline and to let the stitching hang halfway off the edge. (Fig. 13-7)

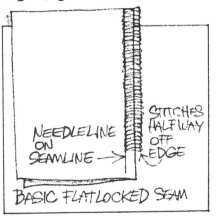

Fig. 13-7: **In flatlock seaming, the serger does not trim the fabric. Guide the edges away from the knives, so the stitches will hang off.**

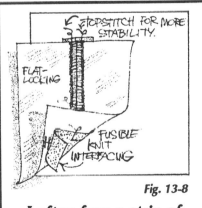

Fig. 13-8

I often fuse a strip of fusible-knit interfacing under the flatlocking. Then, if it is in a high-stress area (such as a shoulder seam or a raglan sleeve), I top-stitch on both sides with the blindhem foot to secure the edges. (Fig. 13-8)

Jan Saunders

For a stronger flatlocked seam, you can use several variations. They're listed here in order from the least stable to the most stable.

Variation 1

Use this method for fabrics that may ravel slightly but not for high-stress garments or seams.

1. Serge-finish both seam allowances using a narrow, balanced, 3-thread stitch, aligning the needle with the seamline and trimming the excess allowance.

2. Then, using a wide stitch, flatlock the edges together. Be sure to let the stitching hang halfway off the edge. (Fig. 13-9)

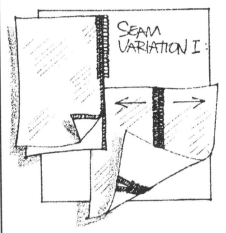

Fig. 13-9: **Serge-finish both edges with a narrow balanced stitch, then flatlock with a wide stitch.**

3. Open the seam and pull the stitching flat.

Variation 2

This method works well for extremely ravelly fabric.

1. Serge-finish the seam allowances and press them to the wrong side. (Fig. 13-10)

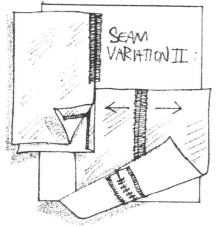

Fig. 13-10: Serge-finish the allowances and press them to the wrong side. Flatlock over the folds.

2. With the folds together, flatlock the seam, allowing the stitches to hang halfway off the edge.

3. Open the seam and pull the stitching flat.

Variation 3

The strongest, most stable flatlocked seam, this variation can be used with ravelly fabric on seams that will experience maximum stress.

1. Serge-finish the allowances and straight-stitch the seam right sides together. (Fig. 13-11)

2. Press the seam open, then fold the fabric wrong sides together along the seamline.

3. Flatlock over the straight-stitched seam, allowing the stitches to hang halfway off the edge. Open the seam and pull the stitching flat.

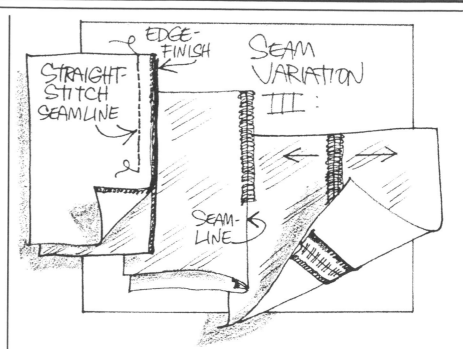

Fig. 13-11: For the strongest flatlocked seam, serge-finish the allowances and straight-stitch the seam. Then flatlock over the seamline.

Reversing the stitch

On any version of the flatlock, **loops are formed on the topside and a ladder is formed on the underside** when the fabric is pulled flat. (Fig. 13-12) However, either side of the flatlocking stitch can be used on the outside of your garment or project.

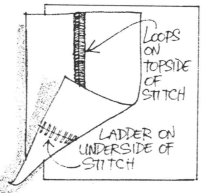

Fig. 13-12: Either side of the flatlocking can be featured on the outside of a garment.

> *In decorative flatlocking, the loops are usually on the right side of the garment. Because the ladder thread has to go through the needle to accomplish this, many heavier decorative threads cannot be used.*
> *Ronda Chaney*

✄ To place the loops on the **outside** of a garment, flatlock the fabric **wrong sides together.**

✄ To place the ladder on the **outside** of the garment, flatlock the fabric **right sides together.**

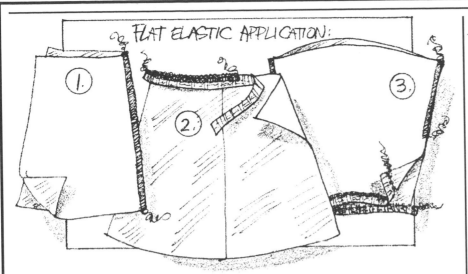

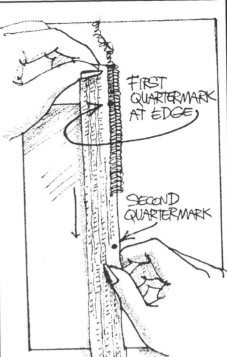

Fig. 13-13: Serge one side seam, apply the elastic, then serge the other side seam.

Fig. 13-15: Stretch the elastic to meet the quartermarks as you flatlock over it.

Flatlocking elastic

Use either a 2- or 3-thread flatlock stitch for bulk-free elastic application—ideal for lingerie.

Note: It's easiest to apply elastic to a flat edge. Serge one side seam, apply the elastic to the waistline, then serge the remaining side seam, trimming off any excess elastic. (Fig. 13-13)

1. When applying elastic to a woven fabric, serge-finish to ravel-proof the fabric edge. Use a narrow, balanced stitch, with the needle on the seamline.

2. Adjust your serger for a long, medium-width, flatlock stitch. The long stitch helps keep the elastic from stretching out of shape. Use matching all-purpose or serger thread or woolly nylon.

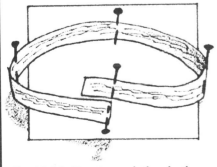

Fig. 13-14: Quartermark the elastic equally, allowing at least 1" extra at the beginning end.

> *To avoid worrying about serging over pins, quartermark using a disappearing marker.*
> **Naomi Baker**

3. Quartermark the elastic and the fabric. (Fig. 13-14) Leave at least 1" extra at the beginning end of the elastic to anchor the serging.

4. Place the fabric and elastic right sides together if you want the ladder on the outside, or put the wrong sides together if you want to feature the loops. Begin serging over the elastic until you reach the first quartermark. Insert the fabric underneath the elastic at that mark. Serge slowly, allowing the stitches to hang off the edge. Stretch the elastic to match up each of the quartermarks as you serge. (Fig. 13-15)

5. Gently pull the stitches flat.

Flatlocking lace

Flatlocking can also be used for neat and bulk-free lace application.

1. If necessary, serge-finish to ravel-proof the fabric edge. Use a narrow, balanced stitch, with the needle on the seamline. Select a rigid lace with at least one straight edge to flatlock over.

> *When you are flatlocking stretch lace, you must also flatlock along a straight edge. For best results, use the previous instructions for flatlocking elastic.*
> **Naomi Baker**

2. Adjust your serger for a basic, medium-width, medium-length, 2- or 3-thread flatlock.

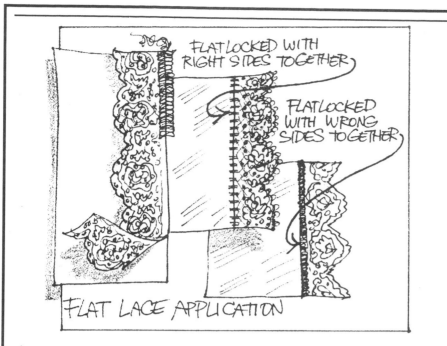

Fig. 13-16: Flatlock with right sides together to show the ladder on the outside. Place wrong sides together to show the loops.

3. Place the lace and fabric together, lining up the edges. With the lace side up, serge the edge, allowing the stitches to hang halfway off. (Fig. 13-16) Serge

3. Place the lace and fabric together, lining up the edges. With the lace side up, serge the edge, allowing the stitches to hang halfway off. (Fig. 13-16) Serge with right sides together to position the ladder stitches on the right side, or with wrong sides together for loops on the outside.

4. Gently pull the seam flat.

Decorative Flatlocking

Any flatlocking can be decorative because one side of the stitching always appears on the right side of the garment or project. By using decorative thread, you can make any flatlocked seam a design element. Or by flatlocking over folds, you can position flatlocking anywhere on the fabric.

Flatlocking over a fold

Flatlock stitching does not have to be on a seamline. Just fold the fabric along any line where you want to place stitching, and flatlock over the fold. Use a 2-, 3-, or 3/4-thread stitch, and guide the fabric so the stitches hang halfway off the edge. (Fig. 13-17) Because the fabric is folded, it will spread out flat under the entire stitch width when pulled flat.

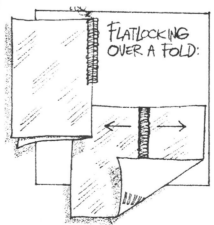

Fig. 13-17: Let the stitches hang off the edge so the fabric spreads out flat under the stitching when it's gently pulled.

> *You'll find it much easier to flatlock a straight-line fold. It's more difficult to fold a curved edge and flatlock along it accurately.*
> *Gale Grigg Hazen*

Using decorative thread

Decorative thread is often used for flatlocking, because at least one side of the stitching will be visible. If the looped side of the stitch will be on the outside of the garment, use decorative thread in the upper looper. If the ladder will be on the outside, use decorative thread in the needle (don't forget that the thread must be small enough to fit through the needle eye).

> *When doing decorative, 3-thread flatlocking with the loops on the right side, I sometimes use monofilament nylon thread in the lower looper so it will be less visible (see Fig. 13-2). When you do this, you will need to loosen the lower looper tension more than for regular flatlocking. If not, the monofilament is so strong that it can prevent the stitches from forming at all.*
> *Naomi Baker*

See Chapter 12 for more information on decorative thread. Remember when you change to a decorative thread, always check your tensions. Adjust them if necessary to perfect the stitch.

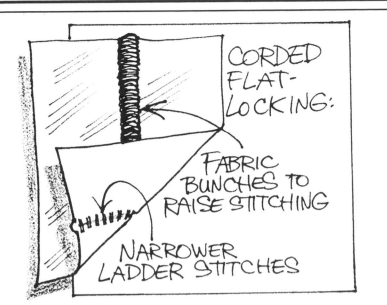

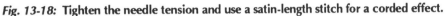

Fig. 13-18: Tighten the needle tension and use a satin-length stitch for a corded effect.

Corded flatlocking

Narrow flatlocking with a short (satin) stitch length can look like piping or corded stitching. For a more corded effect without using filler cord, tighten the needle tension. The ladder stitch on the underside will be narrower, and fabric will collect under the stitch giving it a raised or corded appearance. (Fig. 13-18)

> *Corded flatlocking looks sensational with variegated thread in the upper looper.*
> **Jan Saunders**

Flatlocking over ribbon and other trim

Using the serge-cording technique (see page 99), you can flatlock over any ribbon, trim, or even yarn to add a unique decorative element on any garment fold. Try flatlocking over a ribbon to cover a seamline, too. (Fig. 13-19)

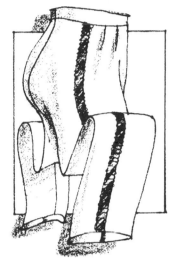

Fig. 13-19: Flatlock a ribbon over a seamline for decorative detailing.

The ribbon or trim must be narrow enough to fit between the needle and the knives so that it won't be cut or stitched through. We recommend 1/4"-wide or narrower ribbon or trim for most serger models. If your stitch is less than 5mm wide, you may need to use 1/8"-wide trim.

1. Adjust your serger for a long, wide, 2- or 3-thread flatlock. "Float" the ribbon or trim on the fabric by using monofilament nylon thread in the upper looper. Or use matching serger or all-purpose thread.

2. Place the ribbon or trim over the front and under the back of the presser foot. If your foot has a tape guide (see page 12), thread it through that. If possible, disengage the knife; otherwise, be careful not to cut the ribbon or trim while serging. Make any tension adjustments if necessary.

3. Hold the ribbon taut in front of and behind the presser foot, and serge over it for about 1". Fold the fabric wrong sides together along the seamline or stitching line.

4. Raise the presser foot and insert the fabric so the fold or seamline is under the center of the ribbon. The ribbon or trim and stitches should both hang halfway off the fabric edge when serged. (Fig. 13-20)

5. Pull the stitches flat so the ribbon or trim lies flat on top of the fabric.

If you're flatlocking using monofilament nylon thread, remember to use a low temperature setting when pressing. Higher temperatures will melt the nylon.
Ruthann Spiegelhoff

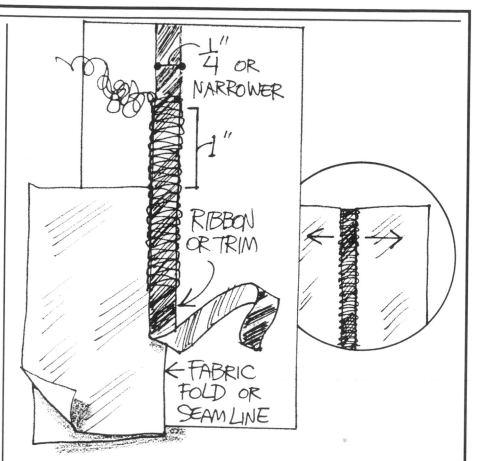

Fig. 13-20: **Anchor flatlocking over ribbon or trim before inserting the fabric. Hang the trim halfway off the edge with the stitching.**

Decorative flatlocking options

As you become more comfortable with decorative flatlocking, you'll learn other possibilities for ornamenting garments and projects. Using a long, narrow flatlock stitch and the serge-cording technique (see page 99), you can attach narrow decorative cording anywhere on your garment or project to simulate piping. (Fig. 13-21) Other options include flatlocking down the center of serged braid (see page 100) and using flatlocking as a base for decorative sewing-machine stitching (see page 102) anywhere on your fabric.

For other decorative flatlocking ideas, see any of the Know Your Serger series books listed on page 144.
Naomi Baker

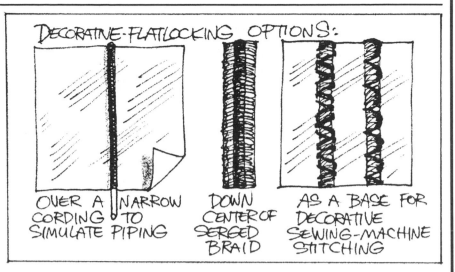

Fig. 13-21: **Flatlocking gives you many additional possibilities for ornamental serging.**

14

Narrow Rolled Edges: Popular and Painless

✂ **Basic Rolled Edges**
✂ **Decorative Rolled Edges**

The narrow rolled edge is one of the most popular serged stitches because it neatly and attractively finishes an edge, rolling the fabric to the underside as it is stitched. The advent of the serger meant that home-sewers could duplicate this durable but delicate factory edge-finish on anything from napkins and home-decorating projects to sportswear and formal wear. (Fig. 14-1)

Basic Rolled Edges

A rolled edge is made with a short, narrow stitch. Because the fabric between the needle and the knives is actually wider than the stitch, the raw edge rolls around a narrow stitch finger to the wrong side, where it's hidden under the stitching. The result is a narrow, corded-looking finish. (Fig. 14-2)

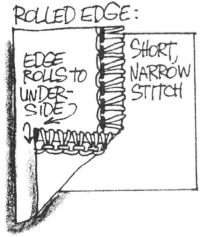

Fig. 14-2: **The narrow stitch wraps the raw edge to the wrong side. The satin length gives it a delicate, corded effect.**

Fig. 14-1: **Serged narrow rolled edges are popular and painless.**

Adjusting for a rolled edge

Adjusting for a rolled edge is not difficult, and once you get some practice, you won't even stop to think about it. You simply need to change the stitch width, stitch length, and tension of a basic 2- or 3-thread stitch—these are all skills you've learned in previous chapters.

Stitch width—(Also see Regulating Stitch Width in Chapter 7.)

✄ For a rolled edge, you'll use a very narrow, needle-like stitch finger so the narrow stitch can roll the fabric around to the underside. Some models have a built-in adjustment (a lever or dial) to change or alter the stitch finger. On other sergers you must change a needle plate, presser foot, or both to switch the stitch finger. Refer to your owner's manual to see which adjustment is needed.

✄ Use only one needle if your serger has two needle positions. It will usually be the right needle, but some models use the left (check your owner's manual).

✄ If your model has the capability, widen the cutting width for heavier fabric, so there's enough seam allowance to roll to the underside.

Stitch length—For many rolled edges, you'll want to use a short (or satin) stitch length so the thread completely covers the edge. See page 95 for more information on adjusting for a satin-length stitch.

> ***For a softer rolled edge, adjust for a length slightly longer than a satin stitch (1.5mm to 2mm, depending on the weight of the fabric). This edge is most often featured on silky or other lightweight fabrics.***
> ***Sue Green-Baker***

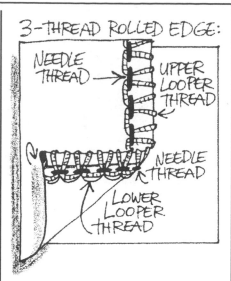

3-THREAD ROLLED EDGE:

Fig. 14-3: **The lower looper tension is tightened to pull the upper looper thread completely to the underside. The edge rolls as the stitches wrap over it.**

Tension adjustment for a 3-thread rolled edge—This is the most common rolled edge, available on practically all models. The lower looper tension is tightened, causing the upper looper thread to wrap around the edge to the underside of the fabric. The fabric edge rolls to the underside as the stitches wrap the edge. (Fig. 14-3)

1. Adjust your serger for a 3-thread rolled edge by tightening the lower looper tension almost completely. Keep the needle and upper looper tensions at their normal settings.

2. Test the stitch. If the upper looper thread doesn't wrap the edge completely, tighten the lower looper tension even more. If that doesn't perfect the stitch, loosen the upper looper tension slightly. (Fig. 14-4) If the fabric puckers along the needleline, loosen the needle tension slightly.

3. Continue testing and adjusting the stitch until the lower looper forms an almost-straight line of stitching on the underside of the fabric and the upper looper completely wraps the edge.

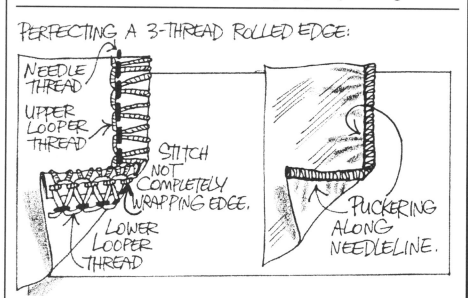

PERFECTING A 3-THREAD ROLLED EDGE:

Fig. 14-4: **Tighten the lower looper tension as much as needed to wrap the upper looper thread to the underside. For additional tightening, loosen the upper lopper tension slightly. If the fabric puckers, loosen the needle tension.**

Tension adjustment for a 2-thread rolled edge—Some models have a 2-thread rolled-edge capability, using the needle thread and one looper thread. The needle thread is tightened, so the looper thread wraps the edge and causes it to roll. (Fig. 14-5) Consult your owner's manual for complete instructions.

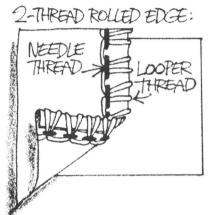

Fig. 14-5: Tighten the needle thread until the looper thread wraps the edge completely.

1. Tighten the needle tension substantially so the needle thread forms a straight line on both sides of the stitch.

2. Loosen the looper tension slightly, if necessary, so the looper thread wraps completely and evenly around the edge of the fabric. (Fig. 14-6)

3. Test and adjust the stitch as needed.

Perfecting the stitch

Because your rolled edge might need some fine-tuning, especially on more difficult fabrics, be sure to test it before cutting out the garment. Use actual project scraps and test on the lengthwise, crosswise, and bias grainlines, following these guidelines:

✂ For the cleanest rolled-edge finish, trim part of the seam allowance while serging. On a slippery, lightweight fabric, you

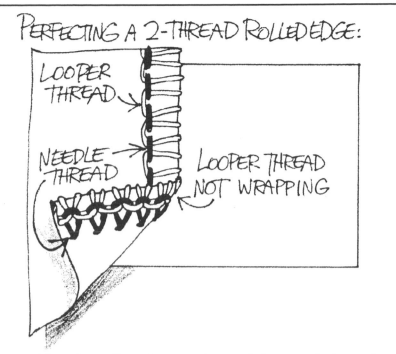

Fig. 14-6: Tighten the needle tension as much as needed to wrap the looper thread completely around the edge. For additional tightening, loosen the looper tension slightly.

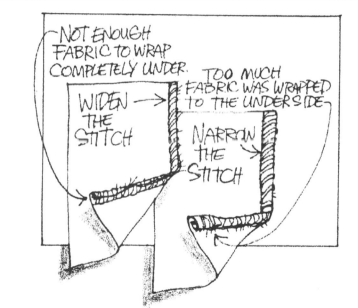

Fig. 14-7: Adjust the stitch width so the correct amount of fabric rolls to the underside.

may need to trim as much as 1/4" to perfect the rolled edge.

✂ Prewash the fabric (unless it's dryclean only) to remove any sizing. Stiff sizing will often prevent the fabric edge from rolling or may cause skipped stitches.

✂ If tiny fibers poke out through the stitching at the edge, widen the stitch. If they poke out on the underside of the stitching, narrow the stitch. (See Fig. 14-7)

Use a strip of water-soluble stabilizer on top of the fabric as you roll the edge. It will stabilize the finish and prevent threads from poking out. Carefully tear or wash away the excess.

Naomi Baker

Is there a portion of the rolled edge that doesn't roll uniformly? This often happens on an intersecting seam or at a change in grain direction. Dab a drop of seam sealant on the wrong side of the unrolled stitching. Let the sealant dry until it's slightly tacky, then finger-press the edge to the wrong side, holding it for a moment to create a permanent bond. (Fig. 14-8)

Gail Brown

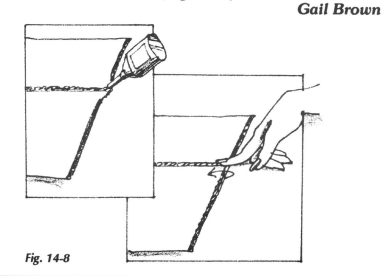

Fig. 14-8

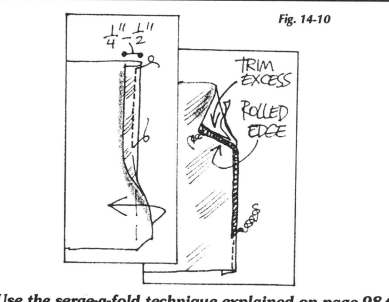

Fig. 14-10

Use the serge-a-fold technique explained on page 98 to perfect a rolled edge on problem fabric. The stitching won't pull away from the edge and no threads can poke out through the stitching. (Fig. 14-10)

Gail Brown

✂ If threads are still poking out, try shortening the stitch to cover the edge more completely.

✂ On sheer or loosely woven fabric, the stitches can pull away from the fabric edge. (Fig. 14-9)

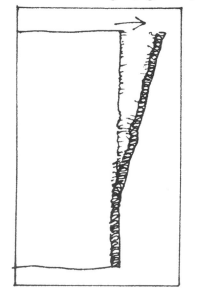

Fig. 14-9: **When stitches pull off the edge, first lengthen the stitch.**

To correct the problem, begin by lengthening the stitch so the needleholes won't perforate the fabric so closely together. If you're still having trouble, widen the stitch slightly or loosen the lower looper tension. Other options are to change the grain of the fabric or choose a different edge-finish.

Rolled-edge seaming

In addition to edge-finishing, the narrow rolled edge can be used for seaming lightweights and sheers, including delicate heirloom laces and fabrics. A rolled-edge seam is not recommended for high-stress areas, but does gives an attractive finish with no seam allowances left to show through to the right side. Simply place the fabric right sides together and serge-seam, using a narrow rolled-edge stitch and trimming the excess seam allowance as you serge. (Fig. 14-11)

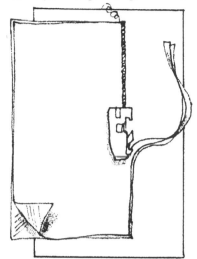

Fig. 14-11: Rolled-edge seaming is ideal for lightweight and sheer fabrics.

For very fragile fabric such as silk, you may need to use fine cotton embroidery thread. Polyester thread is so much stronger than the fibers of the fabric, it rips them as it slides through to make the stitch. These fine cotton threads are not as strong and will snap if you serge too fast.
Gale Grigg Hazen

For a piped effect, place your fabric wrong sides together when rolled-edge seaming. The allowances will be neatly enclosed in the rolled edge on the right side of the garment.
Ronda Chaney

Decorative Rolled Edges

Using decorative thread

Because the upper looper thread is the only visible thread in a 3-thread, rolled-edge stitch, you'll need decorative thread in that position only. You can use serger or all-purpose thread for the needle and lower looper. (On a 2-thread stitch, you'll need it in the looper only.) Be sure to test and adjust the tensions any time you change even one thread.

Any decorative thread (see Chapter 12) can be used for a rolled edge, but there are some favorites. Because **woolly nylon** will fluff up and fill in the spaces between the stitches, it makes the rolled edge easier to perfect. (Fig. 14-12) Because woolly nylon is so

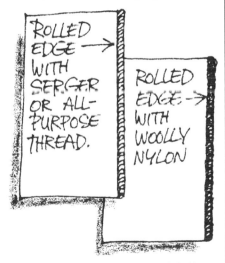

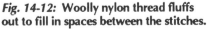

Fig. 14-12: Woolly nylon thread fluffs out to fill in spaces between the stitches.

strong, you need another nylon thread in the lower looper of a 3-thread stitch or the needle of a 2-thread stitch to help wrap the decorative thread completely around the edge. You can use woolly or monofilament nylon thread for this purpose.

Other favorite decorative threads for rolled edges include **rayon**, which gives a luster complementary to silky and dressier fabrics; and **metallic**, which adds a glittery touch.

I automatically use nylon thread in the lower looper for the best 3-thread rolled edge, no matter what thread I have in the upper looper.
Naomi Baker

Always loosen the tension on the woolly nylon so it will fluff out between the stitches in the rolled edge. It needs to be loose enough to relax and spread after the stitch is formed.
Ruthann Spiegelhoff

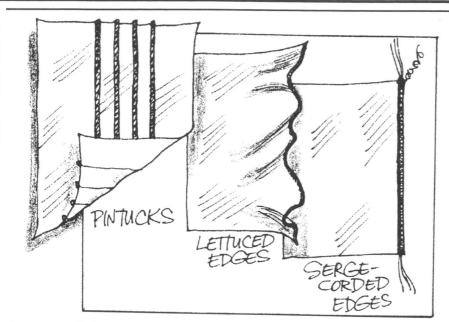

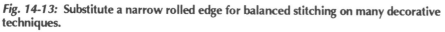

Fig. 14-13: Substitute a narrow rolled edge for balanced stitching on many decorative techniques.

Decorative techniques

A narrow rolled edge can be used for *several* of the decorative balanced-serging applications presented in Chapters 11 and 12. (Fig. 14-13)

✂ *Pintucks*—Follow the serged-tuck guidelines on page 87, substituting a narrow rolled edge for the balanced stitch.

✂ *Lettuced edges*—Use a dainty rolled edge instead of a balanced stitch to lettuce the edge of stretchy knits or bias-cut wovens, following the techniques explained on pages 88 and 89.

✂ *Serge-corded edges*—For a more pronounced, corded rolled edge, insert filler cord under the rolled-edge stitching, using the guidelines on page 99.

Use this technique to make your own **custom-serged piping:**

1. Adjust for a satin-length rolled edge and serge over filler cord onto a precut bias strip such as 1-1/4"-wide *Seams Great.* (Fig. 14-14) Trim about 1/2" as you serge. Serge **slowly** and **do not stretch** as you stitch.

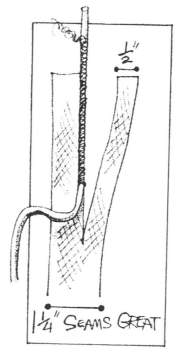

Fig. 14-14: Serge custom piping over bias tricot for insertion into any seamline.

2. Insert the piping into any seamline using the traditional straight-stitching method. Use a piping foot, if available for your serger model, for inserting the piping.

3. *Optional:* Use monofilament nylon thread and a longer stitch if you want to feature the filler itself, such as a decorative metallic cording or a strand of pearls. On some applications, you may find it neater to fold the bias strip lengthwise and serge the piping over the fold.

Also make bouffant, **fishline ruffles** using this same serge-cording technique:

1. Purchase clear **fishing line** from a sporting goods store or other fishing-supply source. Use any weight from the lightweight 12 lb. to heavy 40 lb. line, depending on your fabric weight and desired effect. Use a mediumweight (25 lb.) line for satins and taffetas.

2. Adjust for a short to medium-length rolled-edge stitch. Serge over the fishline on the fabric edge, using the serge-cording technique on page 99. Leave long tails of fishline on both ends of the stitching. Guide the fishline accurately and **serge slowly** to prevent cutting the line. (Fig. 14-15)

3. Stretch the edge to form the ruffles **after** completing the serging. Fishline rolled edges on bias-cut wovens or stretch knits will ruffle most—always test first.

✂ *Serged braids and binding*—Any of the braids and bindings introduced on pages 100 and 101 can be serged with narrow rolled edges instead of balanced stitching. (Fig. 14-16)

✂ *Scalloped edging*—You can sew a more delicate scalloped edge by substituting a narrow rolled edge for the balanced stitch used on page 101.

Fig. 14-15: Use the serge-cording technique to create bouffant, fishline ruffles.

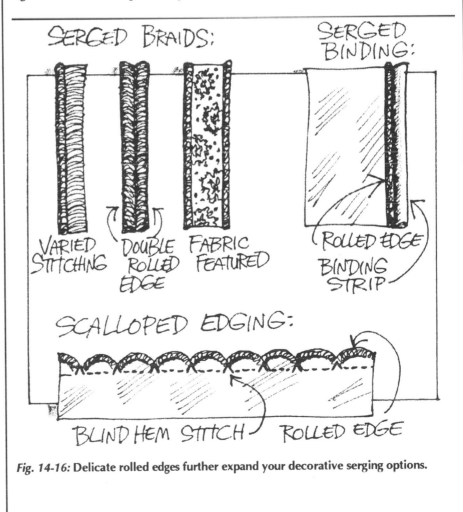

Fig. 14-16: Delicate rolled edges further expand your decorative serging options.

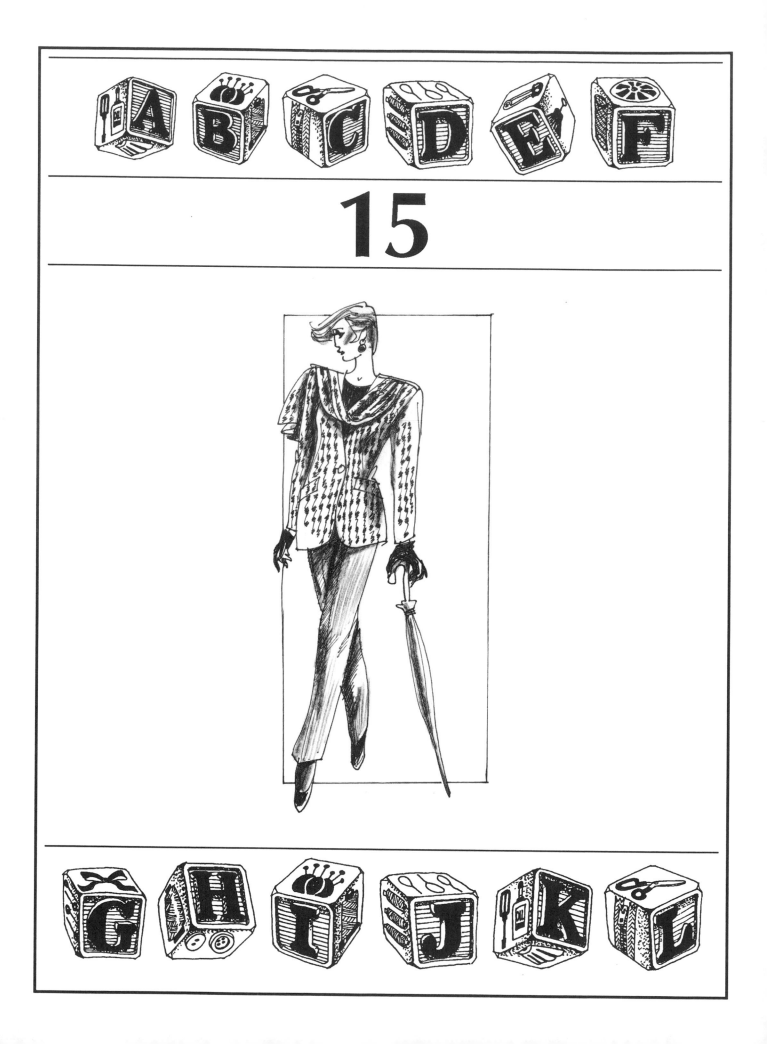

15

Overview of Basic Garment Construction

✂ Fitting
✂ Planning a Strategy
✂ Fast, Flat-construction Serging Order
✂ Common Construction Techniques

Put your serger skills to work to create professionally finished projects quickly and easily. In previous chapters, you've learned many serger techniques. Now you can use this knowledge to simplify garment construction.

Fitting

Always prefit the pattern before cutting out the garment. Because the serged stitch trims the fabric, there isn't always a chance to undo what's already been done after the garment is serged.

1. Recheck your measurements **before** buying a pattern—as often as every six months (or more often if you think you've gained or lost inches). Even without a weight change, body measurements can still change. (Fig. 15-1)

Fig. 15-1: Check your measurements and buy the proper pattern size.

The alterations you'll need to make before serger construction are essentially the same as for sewing. If you need more complicated alterations and lack the experience, refer to one of the many fitting and alteration books now available.

Naomi Baker

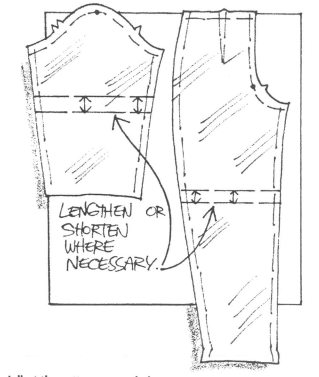

Fig. 15-2: **Adjust the pattern as needed.**

LENGTHEN OR SHORTEN WHERE NECESSARY.

Before cutting out your garment, take some time to plan a serging strategy. This will save valuable construction time and prevent possible mistakes. Read the pattern guidesheet and mark strategy changes in red. For more help, look for a pattern that includes serger tips and guidelines.

> *I enlarge the pattern piece guide from the first page of the instruction sheet. As I go through the pattern, I note on each piece what I plan to do. Then I number the order. This makes cutting out and preparation easier.*
>
> **Gale Grigg Hazen**

What kind of seams, edge-finishes, and hems?

✂ If you want straight-stitched seams or if your garment will require that you fine-tune the fit during construction, plan to serge-finish the allowances, then straight-stitch the seams. Or, straight-stitch the seams, then serge-finish the allowances together after fitting the garment. (See Chapter 9.) Both methods leave the full seam-allowance width for possible fitting adjustments as well as durability.

✂ Quickly serge-finish all the edges continuously. Serge the hem edges first, then the upper edges, leaving 4" to 6" of thread chain between the garment pieces. (Fig.

2. Purchase the pattern size recommended for your measurements and figure type (petite or women's, for example). Determine your figure type by comparing your measurements with those listed in the back of any major pattern catalog. Consider buying two sizes or a multi-sized pattern if your top size is larger or smaller than your pant or skirt size.

3. Adjust the pattern's length measurements if they vary from your own. (Fig. 15-2) Use the back length listed on the pattern when comparing your measurements. (Don't measure the back length of the pattern piece because it may include extra length for ease and blousing.) Measure and compare the actual pattern pieces when adjusting the hem and sleeves.

> *Measure a favorite garment with proportions similar to the garment you wish to make. Check the waist, hip, shoulder line, and sleeve width and depth. Compare these to the pattern. Many patterns have the finished measurements labeled right on the pattern pieces.*
>
> **Gale Grigg Hazen**

4. Adjust the pattern circumference if needed. Compare your bust, waist, and hip measurements to those listed on the back of the pattern envelope, and adjust the areas that differ. The actual circumference of the garment often is different from the listed measurements because the pattern includes wearing and design ease. Don't eliminate the ease or overfit the pattern—it's fairly easy to make a garment smaller during construction but it's impossible to make it much larger!

* LEAVE SLEEVE CAPS, NECKLINES, & ARMSCYES UNFINISHED.

Fig. 15-3: For speedy serge-finishing, continuously stitch the hems and upper edges. Then clip the thread chains and continuously serge the sides.

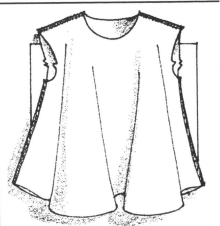

Fig. 15-4: If the fabric is appropriate and fitting isn't critical, serge the seams.

15-3) Clip the thread chains to separate the pieces, then continuously serge-finish the sides. It's unnecessary to serge-finish the armscyes, sleeve caps, or neckline at this time, because they will be finished later during garment construction.

> *You may want to wait and serge-finish some hem edges after you try on the garment. Even with pattern adjustments, the fabric and design may cause a length variation. Waiting also allows you to even up the hem before turning it.*
> **Jan Saunders**

✄ Consider the fabric type and weight and how the seaming method will look and perform on your finished garment. (See Specialty Seaming in Chapter 9.) Test on the actual garment fabric to determine the best option.

✄ If the fabric is appropriate and fitting isn't critical, as for a loose-fitting garment or a pattern you've used previously, serge-seam using one of the methods described on pages 61 through 62. (Fig. 15-4)

✄ If necessary, vary the seaming method on different parts of the garment. You may want specialty seams (see pages 64 – 66) or decorative seams (see pages 97 – 98) only at certain places on the garment. Another consideration is garment closures such as zipper seams.

> *Be sure your pattern has wide enough seam and hem allowances for the serging techniques you'll be using. If not, widen the pattern allowances after making fitting adjustments.*
> **Ruthann Spiegelhoff**

✄ Determine the hemming techniques you'll use for all the edges.

What to serge, what to sew, and in what order?

Define the construction steps you'll take, and arrange them in a time-saving order. Renumber them on your pattern guidesheet. (Fig. 15-5)

✄ Decide what to serge and what to sew. You'll choose to sew tight curves and corners, top-stitching, and conventional zipper applications. Look over the pattern instructions for any other steps that can be converted to serging.

✄ Consolidate similar tasks so you're not switching back and forth between the sewing machine, the serger, and the ironing board. Do as many steps as you can at each position.

✄ Avoid rethreading and readjusting your serger by consolidating as many tasks as you can that require the same serged stitch or thread.

✄ Convert the pattern to the fast, flat-construction serging order, explained next.

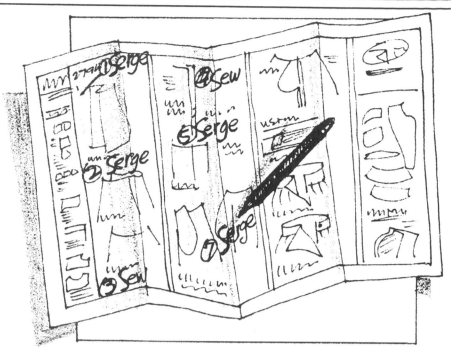

Fig. 15-5: **Plan your serging strategy. Mark construction changes and renumber the steps in a time-saving order.**

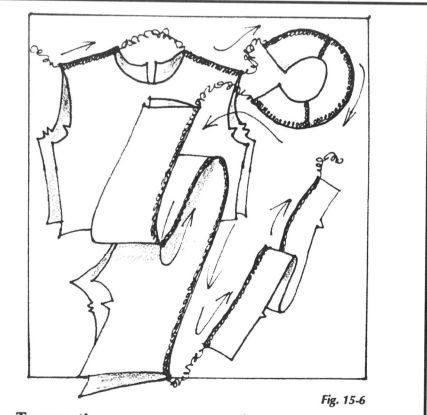

Fig. 15-6

To save time, serge as many edges or seams as you can continuously, without raising the presser foot. (Fig. 15-6) Leave about 4" of thread chain between each seam or edge and clip the thread chains later to separate the sections.

Gail Brown

Fast, Flat-construction Serging Order

When you use a serger, you can easily borrow fast, ready-to-wear production techniques. By serge-finishing and serge-seaming edges while they're still flat, you'll have an easier time handling the fabric and you'll reduce your sewing time. Think through the construction order to serge as many seams and edges as possible while they're still flat.

> *Even if you buy a pattern that includes serger instructions, it won't always include a flat-construction order. You still may need to plan your strategy and mark the serging order on the pattern guidesheet.*
> **Ronda Chaney**

Use the following serging orders to construct basic garments. Modify the steps when using other serging techniques.

Flat-serged top
(Fig. 15-7)

Fig. 15-7: Convert the construction order of a basic pullover top for fast, flat finishing and seaming.

Convert any basic pullover top for fast, flat construction. This serging order works well for knits, but can be used for any oversized woven pullover as well.

1. Serge-seam one shoulder. (Fig. 15-8)

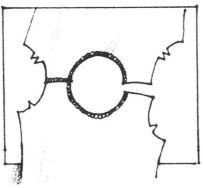

Fig. 15-8: Serge-seam one shoulder and finish the neckline edge.

2. Finish the neckline. This may be serge-finished, bound, or rib-trimmed.

> *When applying ribbing, note that the center front and back and opposite side seams are not actual quarter divisions. Always measure accurately. Before serging the second shoulder seam closed, apply a dab of glue stick to the ribbing to make sure the ends match at the neck edge.*
> **Ruthann Spiegelhoff**

3. Serge-seam the other shoulder, continuing the stitching through the binding or ribbing. (Fig. 15-9)

4. Serge-finish the sleeve edges.

5. Serge-seam the sleeves to the garment.

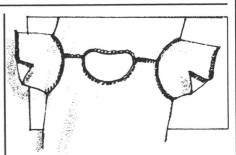

Fig. 15-9: Serge-seam the remaining shoulder. Serge-finish the lower sleeve edges, then serge-seam the sleeves to the armscyes.

6. Serge one sleeve/side seam. (Fig. 15-10)

Fig. 15.10: Serge one sleeve/side seam. Serge-finish the hem edge, then serge the other sleeve/side seam.

7. Serge-finish the hem edge.

8. Serge the other sleeve/side seam.

9. If the neckline was serge-finished, turn and top-stitch the edge to the wrong side. Turn and top-stitch the lower sleeve and hem edges also. (See Quick-serged Items later in this chapter.)

> *On some neckline finishes, the seam allowance may peek out at the neckline edge when the second shoulder seam is serged. If it does, hand tack it so it won't show.*
> **Sue Green-Baker**

Speedy serged blouse
(Fig. 15-11)

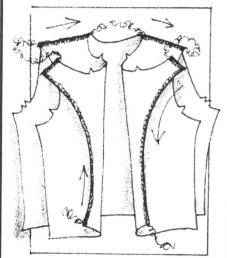

Fig. 15-11: **Use as many flat-construction techniques as possible for basic blouses and one-piece dresses.**

This serging order is ideal for a collared blouse with a button-front closure, but can be used for blouses or one-piece dresses with any type of closure or neckline finish:

1. Continuously serge-seam the shoulders and serge-finish the outer edges of the facings. (Fig. 15-12)

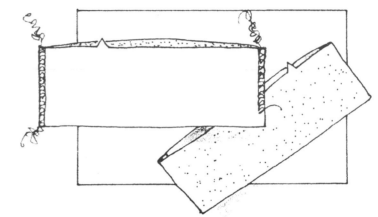

Fig. 15-13: **Serge-seam the collar and facing to the neckline.**

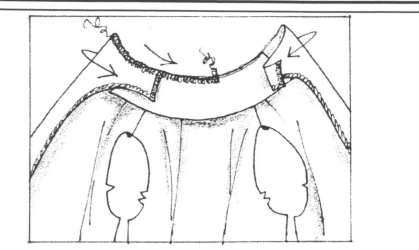

Fig. 15-14: **Make the cuffs.**

Fig. 15-12: **Continuously serge-seam the shoulders and serge-finish the outside facing edges.**

2. Straight-stitch the collar seams, and turn it right side out. (You can use the technique you'll learn for wrapping corners later in this chapter if your pattern has separate top and bottom pieces.)

3. Serge-seam the collar and facing to the neckline. (Fig. 15-13) If your pattern doesn't have a collar, finish the neckline and closure opening at this time. (For example, you may need to attach a facing or insert a zipper.)

4. Apply sleeve plackets, following the instructions on page 76.

5. Serge-seam the sides. Then, without cutting the thread chain, serge-seam the underarms.

6. Serge-seam the cuff ends and turn the cuffs right side out. (Fig. 15-14)

7. Place the right side of the cuff against the right side of the sleeve (Fig. 15-15), and wrap the placket edges toward the underside of the cuff.

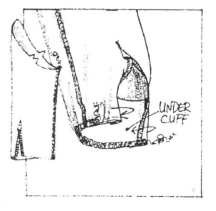

Fig. 15-15: **Serge-seam the cuffs to the sleeves, wrapping the placket edges to the underside.**

8. Serge-seam the cuffs to the sleeves through all layers. (When you extend the cuff, the allowances will automatically wrap to the underside.)

9. Serge the sleeves to the armscyes, lapping the beginning and end of the stitching. (Fig. 15-16) Serge with the garment on top, so the serger can help ease in the sleeve.

10. Serge-finish the lower edge and hem or top-stitch it in place.

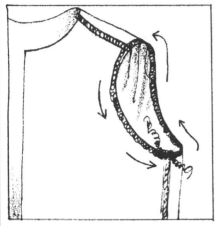

Fig. 15-16: Serge-seam the sleeves to the armscyes, lapping the stitching.

> *If you have a high sleeve cap that needs gathering, use differential-feed or tension gathering (see page 81) to quickly ease the fullness before serging it into the armscye.*
> **Ruthann Spiegelhoff**

11. Tack the facings to the inside, sew buttonholes, attach buttons, and top-stitch the edges, if desired.

Fig. 15-17: Use fast construction techniques to serge a basic skirt.

Basic serged skirt
(Fig. 15-17)

Use this serging order for a four-gored skirt with a sewn-on waistband and zipper closure. Modify the steps for other pattern styles. For a pull-on skirt, use the waistband technique outlined in the serged, pull-on pants, following. If your skirt has pockets, see page 135.

1. Continuously serge-finish the unnotched waistband and center back edges. (Fig. 15-18)

> *Always start serging from the bottom of a skirt or pants. I have serged from the top down by mistake and really stretched out the seamline. Now I'm always careful to serge from the bottom up whenever possible.*
> **Jan Saunders**

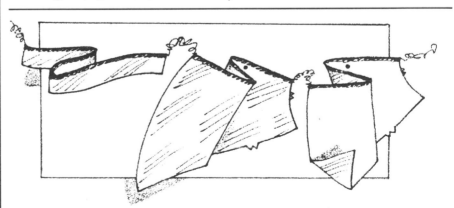

Fig. 15-18: Continuously serge-finish the waistband and center back edges.

2. Straight-stitch the center back seam and apply the zipper.

3. Serge the center front and one side seam. (Fig. 15-19)

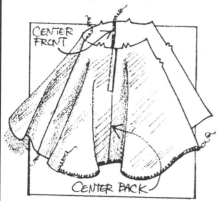

Fig. 15-19: **Serge-seam the center front and one side seam. Serge-finish the hem edge.**

4. Serge-finish the hem edge.

5. Serge the other side seam.

6. Serge-seam the unfinished waistband edge to the skirt, continuing to the end of the underlap. (Fig. 15-20)

7. Serge the waistband ends, and turn the band right side out, tucking the serged allowances into the underlap and over the tops of the zipper teeth. Top-stitch along the seamline to secure, continuing to the end of the underlap. (Fig. 15-21)

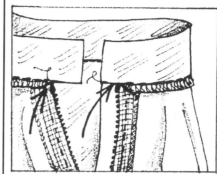

Fig. 15-21: **Turn the waistband right side out and top-stitch next to the seamline.**

8. Blind stitch or top-stitch the lower edge (see Fig. 15-33).

Serged pull-on pants

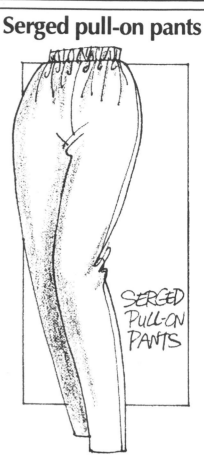

Fig. 15-22: **Use this basic elastic waistline for pull-on skirts as well as easy-to-serge pants.**

For basic pull-on pants with 1-1/4" to 1-1/2"-wide, sew-through elastic in a foldover casing, use this fast and simple serging order. The same waistline technique can be used for a speedy pull-on skirt. Before beginning, cut out the garment with a waistline seam allowance double the width of the elastic. If your pants have in-seam pockets, see page 135.

1. Serge-seam the fronts to the backs along the outside seamlines.

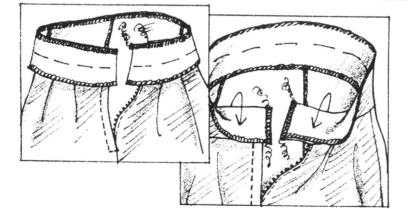

Fig. 15-20: **Serge-seam the waistband to the skirt, then serge-seam the waistband ends.**

2. Serge-finish the bottom hem edges with the outseam allowance toward the back. (Fig. 15-23)

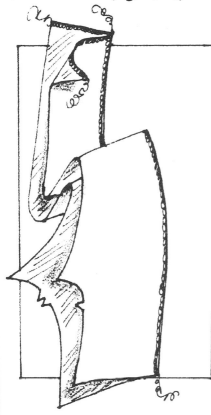

Fig. 15-23: Serge-seam the fronts to the backs along the outside seamlines. Serge-finish the hem edges.

3. Serge the inseams.

4. Serge the crotch seam. To reduce bulk, press the inseams in opposite directions. (Fig. 15-24)

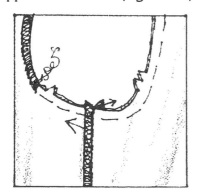

Fig. 15-24: Serge the crotch seam, alternating the inseam direction for less bulk.

5. Measure the elastic comfortably around your waist (about 2" less than your waistline measurement). Sew it into a circle by overlapping the ends and zigzagging.

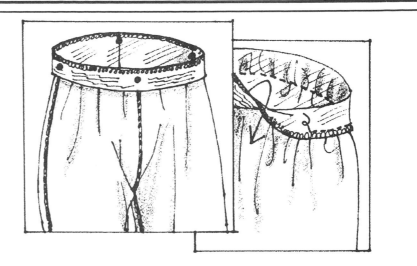

Fig. 15-25: Quartermark and serge-seam the elastic to the top edge. Turn the elastic to the inside and straight-stitch along the lower edge, stretching as you sew.

Quartermark the elastic and the waistline edge. Serge-seam the elastic to the wrong side of the waistline edge (with the elastic on top), matching the quartermarks. (Fig. 15-25)

6. Turn the elastic toward the inside of the pants. Straight-stitch through all layers along the bottom edge of the elastic, stretching as you sew. Then stitch-in-the-ditch at the side seams.

Optional: Top-stitch several evenly spaced rows through the waistband, about 1/4" apart. Steam well to shrink the elastic to its original length.

7. Hem or top-stitch the lower edges.

> *When top-stitching several rows on the elastic, use less elastic (about 3" less than your waistline measurement) and a longer stitch length.*
> **Ruthann Spiegelhoff**
>
> *If you use elastic thread in the bobbin for top-stitching the waistband, it helps minimize the stretching and looks great!*
> **Jan Saunders**

Common Construction Techniques

The list of serger construction techniques is practically endless—you've just learned several under Fast, Flat-construction Serging Order and there are others throughout this book. Most were created by converting popular conventional techniques to time-saving, serger strategies. As your serging skills advance, you'll learn many more and select your favorites. Here we'll outline a few that we use most often.

> *For more serger construction techniques, see Other Books by the Authors in the back of this book. Innovative Serging and Simply Serge Any Fabric will be most helpful.*
> **Naomi Baker**

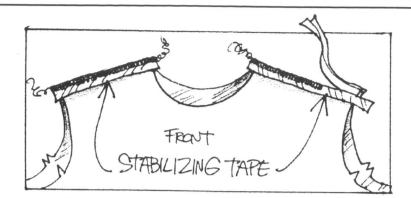

Fig. 15-26: Stabilize stretch-prone seams by serging over a tape.

Reinforced seams

Stretch-prone seams, such as shoulders and waistlines, need to be stabilized, because the serged stitch can stretch. On very stretchy knits or bias wovens, you may also need to stabilize neckline or skirt seams.

Serge over *Seams Great,* twill tape, or a strip of fusible interfacing to stabilize a seam. Your choice will depend on the fabric weight and results you're looking for, so always test first.

> *For a quick, stable seam, I serge over clear elastic. Do not stretch the elastic as you sew.*
> *Ruthann Spiegelhoff*

For a shoulder seam, place the fabric right sides together with the front on top. Put the stabilizing tape over the seamline (or fuse on a strip of interfacing). Serge-seam through all layers with the needle on the seamline. Press the allowances toward the back. (Fig. 15-26)

Wrapping corners

When corners are serge-seamed and turned to the inside (such as on collar points and cuffs), excess fabric can cause a lump at the point. To prevent that, wrap one serged seam allowance toward the garment before serging the other side of the corner.

1. Serge-seam one side of the corner with right sides together.

2. Press the seam flat, then wrap and press the allowance back toward one side of the fabric. (Fig. 15-27)

3. Serge the other side of the corner, stitching over the folded seam allowance. Press the seams flat, turn the corner right side out, and press again. (Fig. 15-28)

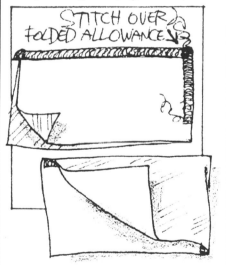

Fig. 15-28: Serge the other side of the corner. Press and turn right side out.

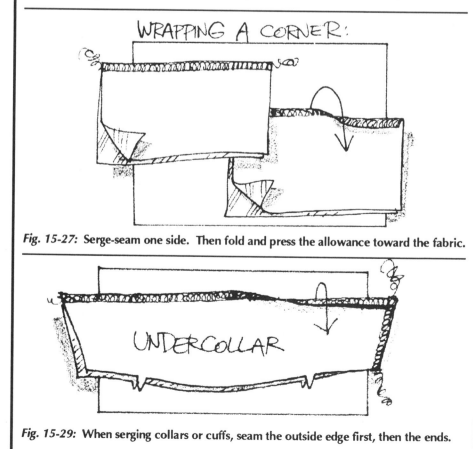

Fig. 15-27: Serge-seam one side. Then fold and press the allowance toward the fabric.

Fig. 15-29: When serging collars or cuffs, seam the outside edge first, then the ends.

Note: When sewing cuffs and collars, serge the outside seam first, fold the allowance toward the facing or undercollar, then serge the ends, stitching over the folded allowance. (Fig. 15-29)

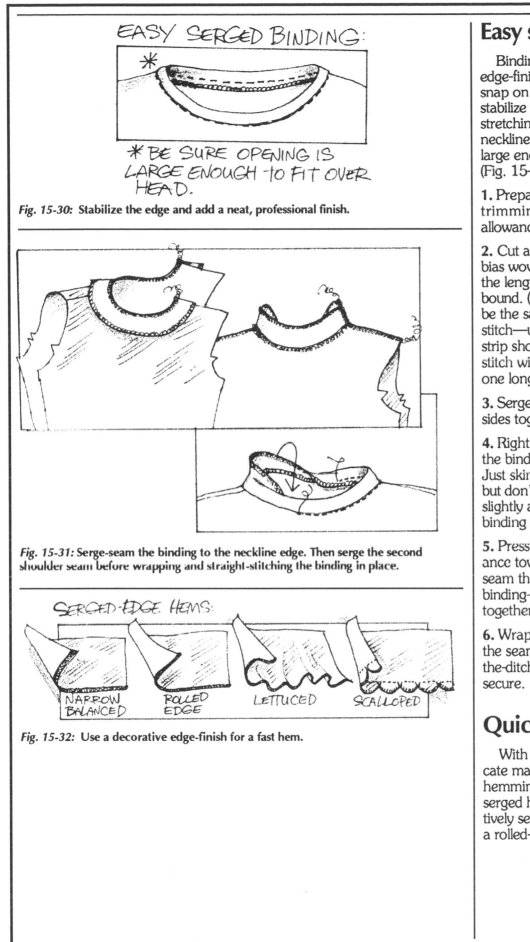

EASY SERGED BINDING:

* BE SURE OPENING IS LARGE ENOUGH TO FIT OVER HEAD.

Fig. 15-30: Stabilize the edge and add a neat, professional finish.

Fig. 15-31: Serge-seam the binding to the neckline edge. Then serge the second shoulder seam before wrapping and straight-stitching the binding in place.

SERGED-EDGE HEMS:

NARROW BALANCED   ROLLED EDGE   LETTUCED   SCALLOPED

Fig. 15-32: Use a decorative edge-finish for a fast hem.

Easy serged binding

Binding is a neat, professional edge-finish that you can do in a snap on the serger. It will also stabilize the edge and eliminate stretching. Before binding a neckline, be sure the opening is large enough to fit over your head. (Fig. 15-30)

1. Prepare the neckline edge by trimming off the seam allowances.

2. Cut a 1"-wide binding strip of bias woven or crossgrain knit fabric the length of the edge to be bound. (The finished binding will be the same width as the serged stitch—usually 1/4". The binding strip should be three times the stitch width plus 1/4".) Serge-finish one long edge of the strip.

3. Serge-seam one shoulder, right sides together.

4. Right sides together, serge-seam the binding strip to the neckline. Just skim the edge with the knives, but don't trim. (Fig. 15-31) Stretch slightly around the curves so the binding will lie flat.

5. Press the neckline seam allowance toward the binding. Serge-seam the second shoulder and binding-strip ends, right sides together.

6. Wrap the binding firmly around the seam allowance and stitch-in-the-ditch from the right side to secure.

Quick-serged hems

With the serger, we can duplicate many popular ready-to-wear hemming techniques. The fastest serged hem is made by decoratively serging the edge, usually with a rolled-edge or narrow balanced stitch. (Fig. 15-32) Use a lettuced edge (pages 88 and 89) or a scalloped edge (page 101) for novelty detailing.

> **To stabilize a hem edge, serge over pearl cotton, ribbon, or narrow twill tape. If you are using a sweater knit, unravel a length of yarn and serge over that. If you want to have stretch and recovery on a hem edge, serge over elastic cord, a double strand of elastic thread, or clear elastic.**
>
> **Jan Saunders**

Serged and turned hems are also simple and easy. Serge-finish the edge, then turn the hem allowance to the wrong side and top-stitch it in place using a straight-stitch, twin-needle, or zigzag. (Fig. 15-33) For a hidden hem, blind-stitch it in place from the wrong side. On sheers, serge, turn twice, and top-stitch.

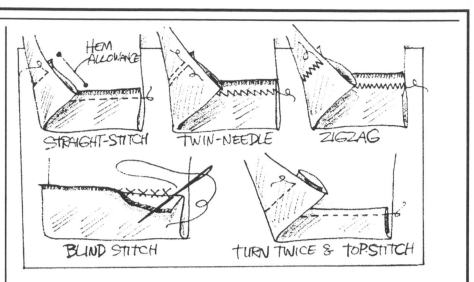

Fig. 15-33: Serged and turned hems are used on many garments.

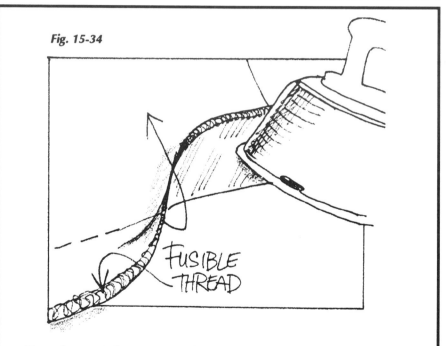

Fig. 15-34

FUSIBLE THREAD

> **For the quickest turned hem, serge-finish with fusible thread (see page 92) in the lower looper. Then simply turn and fuse the hem in place. (Fig. 15-34)**
>
> **Gail Brown**

Serged pockets

For the easiest serged **patch pocket,** decoratively serge-finish the edges from the right side and top-stitch it in position on the garment. (Fig. 15-35) Either stabilize the top edge of the pocket as you decoratively serge it, or serge-finish and turn a hem to the right or wrong side before serging the sides.

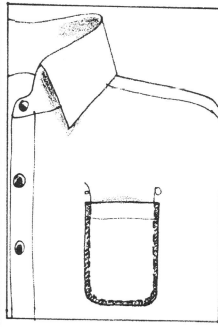

Fig. 15-35: Serge-finished and top-stitched patch pockets are fast and easy.

In-seam pockets can be easily serged when you are constructing pants or a skirt:

1. If the pockets are not part of the garment piece, serge-seam the pocket pieces to the allowances on both sides of the seam.

SERGED IN-SEAM POCKET:

MACHINE BASTING

3" – 4"

Fig. 15-36: Straight-stitch on the seamline, machine basting between the opening dots. Serge-seam from the hemline, curving around the outer pocket edge.

2. Straight-stitch from the waistline to the top of the pocket opening. Back-stitch to secure, then machine-baste to the lower edge of the pocket opening, as shown. (Fig. 15-36) Return to a normal stitch length, back-stitch again, and straight-stitch for an additional 3" to 4".

> *With more serging experience, you can skip the machine-basted section on many fabrics. You'll be able to serge quickly around the curved pocket edges and won't have to stop and remove the basting stitches afterward.*
> *Naomi Baker*

3. Beginning at the hemline, serge-seam the sides and around the outside edge of the pocket.

4. Press the pockets toward the front before finishing the waistline edge.

5. Carefully remove the machine basting to open the pocket.

Simple belt loops

Several types of belt loops can be made quickly and easily on the serger. Use one that will look compatible with your garment. (Fig. 15-37)

✂ **Thread-chain loops**—Adjust your serger for a short, narrow stitch or a rolled edge and serge off a length of thread chain. Using a large-eyed needle, stitch sections of the chain securely in place for each belt loop. Also use thread-chain loops for small buttons or the eye portion of a hook and eye.

✂ **Serge-finished loops**—For quick, fabric belt loops, decoratively serge-finish the outer edges of a long strip, using a short, narrow stitch or a rolled edge. Use a double-layer strip for lightweight fabric. Cut the strip into sections for the loops, and sew them to your garment.

✂ **Edge-stitched loops**—Serge-finish one long edge of a strip measuring three times the width you want your belt loops. Fold the strip into thirds, and edge-stitch both sides. Cut the loops from the strip, and sew them to your garment. (Fig. 15-38)

> *For ravel-free ends, mark the loop cutting lines on the strip and apply seam sealant on each line. Allow it to dry before cutting the loops.*
> *Sue Green-Baker*

Fig. 15-37: **Serge belt loops to complement your garment.**

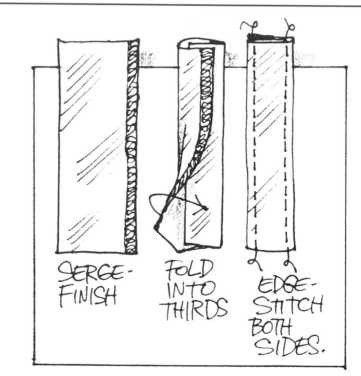
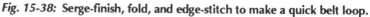

Fig. 15-38: **Serge-finish, fold, and edge-stitch to make a quick belt loop.**

Appendices

Serger Care and Maintenance

Your serger is a finely tuned piece of equipment. Regular cleaning and oiling can prevent many serging problems and extend the life of your machine. Even with careful use and maintenance, a serger should be checked and retimed by a serger repair specialist at least once a year.

Follow these basic guidelines to keep your serger running smoothly:

✂ *Clean the lint and trimmings from your machine after every garment or project.* Disengage the knife and remove the needle plate. Use a stiff-bristled brushed dipped sparingly in sewing machine oil to remove lint particles and gently lubricate the machine workings.

✂ *Change the needles at least every third project* or more often if necessary. Use the correct type and size of needles and insert them correctly, following the instructions in your owner's manual. They must be pushed completely up into the needle bar and screwed in securely, and the groove on the shaft must be squarely to the front.

✂ *Oil the machine after every 12 to 15 hours of serging.* Check your owner's manual for oiling instructions (some models won't need oiling), and use sewing machine oil only. Always oil your serger immediately if it is noisier than usual or hasn't been used for several months. After oiling, serge a few inches on absorbent scrap fabric to remove any excess oil.

✂ *Once a month, check the knives and clean the serger thoroughly.* Test whether the knives are cutting smoothly by serging on slippery, lightweight fabric. If not, replace the softer blade according to your owner's manual. (One replacement blade usually comes with the new machine.) Remove the lint from the machine workings as previously described. Clean between the tension discs with a knotted thread (put a tiny amount of oil on it). Jan Saunders also suggests using the edge of a dollar bill to clean the inset type tension discs—it won't rip, and the fibers, with oil from handling, will draw out the lint. Also remove any built-up machine oil with rubbing alcohol on a cotton swab or soft cloth.

Serger Troubleshooting

Having trouble perfecting your serging? The problem is usually something you can remedy yourself without consulting a repair specialist. Quickly check the most likely possibilities:

1. **Check the obvious.** Is the machine plugged in and turned on? Are the covers closed? Is the presser foot lowered? Have you raised the thread guide pole to its highest position?

2. **Look at the threading.** One of the most common causes of stitching problems is the threading or rethreading. (See Threading Troubleshooting in Chapter 4.)

3. **Examine the needle(s).** Some repair specialists do this the very first thing.

✂ Are you using the exact needle type specified for your serger model? If not, you will likely have stitching problems or stitches won't form at all.

✂ Is the needle inserted correctly, all the way into the needle bar with the groove squarely in the front? If not, the stitches will be irregular or won't form at all. Tighten the set screw so the needle doesn't slip out of position.

✂ Is the needle burred, bent, or dull? If so, you may get puckering, snagging, or skipped stitches. Even a new needle can be defective.

✂ Are you using the correct needle size? For heavy fabric or thread, you may need a larger needle. For delicate fabric and fine thread, a smaller needle will work best.

4. **Is your tension adjustment correct?** If your needle-thread tension is too tight, it can cause puckering or the thread will break. If the looper tensions aren't adjusted correctly, the stitching can be unbalanced, irregular, or puckered. When you change thread or fabric, always check the tension settings and readjust if necessary.

5. **Are the knives dull or out of position?** Test them by serging a piece of slippery, lightweight fabric. If the cutting is ragged and uneven, the softer blade should be replaced. Also check to see if the blades are properly engaged. Refer to your owner's manual for specific instructions or ask your dealer to demonstrate correct positioning if you are unsure.

6. **Are the differential feed and presser-foot pressure adjusted correctly?** Have you returned to a normal setting after serging a heavy, light, or stretchy fabric? Can you use either control to help prevent stretching or puckering (see Chapter 8)?

7. **Have you used the correct serging techniques?**

✂ Are you feeding fabric through the machine correctly? Pulling the fabric through the machine as you serge can cause needle breakage, looper damage, and problems.

On difficult fabrics, have you lifted the toe or the entire foot to insert the fabric under it to begin serging? This can prevent bunching of the thread and will start two layers feeding evenly.

✂ With slippery or heavy fabrics, are you holding the thread chain behind the presser foot to help start serging smoothly? If not, the stitches can bunch or jam under the foot.

✂ Are you using a high-quality, evenly twisted thread for best results? The weight should also be appropriate for the fabric. Some novelty threads cannot be used successfully on all brands and models of sergers, so always test first.

8. **Are you using the right stitch length?** A long stitch might cause puckering and a short stitch can cause stretching or jamming. Always test first before serging your garment or project.

9. Have you regularly cleaned and oiled the machine? See Care and Maintenance (page 138) for specific suggestions.

10. Is your serger completely jammed? Removing the jam without damaging the fabric can be a delicate task. Use this procedure recommended by expert problem solver Sue Green-Baker:

✄ Remove the presser foot and disengage the knife (if possible).

✄ Cut the needle and upper looper threads close to the stitching. Then pull slack in the lower looper thread by tugging underneath the tension control.

✄ Rotate the handwheel back and forth to loosen the needle from the fabric. Raise the needle (if you can) and gently pull on the fabric until it is loosened. Pull the fabric toward the back of the machine, removing it from the stitch finger.

✄ If you can't raise the needle, loosen the needle screw and rotate the handwheel to bring the needle bar up.

✄ Gently remove the needle and loosen the fabric from the stitch finger.

To avoid a jam:

✄ Never serge with the fabric edge to the right of the needle plate when the knives are disengaged. Because the extra fabric isn't trimmed, it can bunch in the stitches or jam in the loopers.

✄ Draw the thread chain toward the back of the machine before stitching.

✄ Keep the looper cover closed while stitching. Trimmings can get caught and tangled in the loopers.

✄ When serging with heavy thread in the looper(s), begin with a medium-length stitch and shorten gradually. The thread bulk can cause a jam if the stitch is too short.

✄ The fabric may be too thick to feed smoothly through the serger. If so, zigzag along the stitching line first to compress the layers.

Glossary of Serging Terms

All-purpose or serger thread—All-purpose thread is usually cotton-covered polyester, wound parallel on conventional spools. Standard serger thread has the same fiber content but is lighter in weight than all-purpose thread and is cross-wound on cones or tubes so that it can feed more easily during high-speed serger sewing.

Balanced stitch—A serged stitch in which the upper- and lower-looper thread tensions are balanced so the threads meet at the edge of the fabric, forming loops.

Binding—A strip of fabric sewn to an edge, then wrapped around it and secured to hide the seam and the raw edge.

Bite—The distance between the knife and the needle, affecting the amount of fabric in the stitch.

Decorative seam (also decorative exposed seam)—Any seam on the outside of a garment or project that enhances design detail.

Decorative thread (also decorative serging or decorative finish)—Any thread other than all-purpose or serger thread, although even a contrasting color of these threads is technically considered decorative. Our favorite decorative threads include woolly nylon, rayon, pearl cotton, metallic, and crochet thread. Many others are also available.

Ease plus—A manual option to the differential feed, accomplished by force-feeding fabric under the front of the presser foot and preventing it from exiting out the back.

Edge-stitch—A medium-length (10 to 12 stitches per inch) straight-stitch on a conventional sewing machine applied near an edge. Edge-stitching is often used to join two serge-finished layers.

Filler cord—Crochet thread, pearl cotton, or buttonhole twist that simulates piping when serged over with a short, satin-length stitch.

Flatlocking—A technique in which the needle thread is loose enough that the serged stitches flatten out on top of the fabric, forming decorative loops when the fabric is pulled apart. The underside will show a ladder effect of evenly spaced, double parallel stitches. Used for both seaming and decorative stitching on a folded edge, flatlocking lends many creative possibilities.

Heavy thread—Crochet thread, pearl cotton, or buttonhole twist used for serge-gathering or filler cord in serger piping.

Long stitch—A serged stitch 4mm or 5mm in length.

Machine basting—Long (6 to 8 stitches per inch) straight-stitching on a conventional sewing machine.

Mail order—A growing trend that offers the convenience of at-home catalog shopping. Almost any product is available through mail order, but without the immediate, hands-on selection available at your local fabric store.

Matching thread—Thread the same color as (or that blends well with) the project fabric.

Medium-length stitch—A serged stitch about 3mm in length.

Medium-width stitch—A serged stitch about 3.5mm wide.

Narrow-width stitch—A serged stitch 2mm to 3mm wide. Used to serge a narrow seam or edge.

Quartermark—Marking a circle or edge in four equal sections, using pins or a disappearing marking pen. This technique is often used to apply elastic evenly.

Ready-to-wear—Garments available for purchase through retail stores and mail-order outlets.

Rolled edge (finish or seam)—Also called a narrow rolled edge or hem, this stitch is created by altering the tension so that the raw edge rolls to the underside. A short stitch length creates an attractive satin-stitch edge.

Same grain—The direction your fabric is being serged—with the lengthwise grain, crosswise grain, or on the bias. Always test a decorative serged stitch on scraps using the same grain as the edges or seams you'll be serging in the project.

Satin stitch (satin length)—A stitch short enough that the thread covers the entire fabric over which it is serged. Appropriate for both a balanced stitch or a rolled edge.

Serge-finishing—Most often a medium-length, medium-width, and balanced 3- or 4-thread stitch used to finish the edge of one layer during the construction process.

Serge-gathering—Several serger techniques are possible for gathering an edge. You can use differential feed on the 2.0 setting. Another option is to tighten your needle tension and lengthen your stitch. Or simply serge over heavy thread with a balanced stitch, being careful not to catch the heavy thread in the serging. Then, after anchoring one end, pull the heavy thread to gather the edge to any specific length. A fourth option is to loosen the needle tension, serge, and then pull up the needle thread.

Serge-seaming—The same medium-length, medium-width, and balanced 3- or 4-thread stitching used for serge-finishing, but in this case it's used to seam two layers together.

Short stitch—A serged stitch 2mm or less in length.

Stitch-in-the-ditch—Stitching directly on top of a previous seamline to secure another layer positioned on the underside. Often used for nearly invisible stitching when applying a binding to an edge.

Straight-stitch—A medium-length (10 to 12 stitches per inch) straight stitch on a conventional sewing machine.

Thread chain—The joined loops formed by serging on a properly threaded machine with no fabric.

Top-stitch—A conventional-machine straight-stitch (10 to 12 stitches per inch) used to attach one layer (often serge-finished) to another or to secure hems and edges.

Wide stitch—A serged stitch 5mm or more in width.

Woolly nylon—One of our favorite decorative threads that became popular with the advent of serger sewing. A crimped nylon thread, it fluffs out to fill in any see-through spaces on a decorative edge.

Zigzag stitch—A basic stitch on a conventional sewing machine that forms a back-and-forth pattern.

Reliable Mail-order Sources

Aardvark Adventures, P.O. Box 2449, Livermore, CA 94551, 415/443-2687. Books, beads, buttons, bangles, plus an unusual assortment of related products. Decorative serging thread, including metallics. Newspaper/catalog, $2.

A Great Notion Sewing Supply, Ltd. 13847-17A Avenue, White Rock, BC V4A 7H4, Canada, 604/538-2829. Hard-to-find sewing supplies. Catalog, $1.

Clotilde, Inc., 1909 S.W. First Ave., Ft. Lauderdale, FL 33315, 800/772-2891 or 305/761-8655. Catalog of over 1,200 items, including special serger threads and other sewing notions and supplies. Free color catalog ($1 for first-class shipping).

Madeira Marketing Ltd., 600 E. 9th St., Michigan City, IN 46360, 219/873-1000. This company carries a wide range of its own decorative threads. $30 minimum. Free brochure.

Nancy's Notions, Ltd., P.O. Box 683, Beaver Dam, WI 53916, 800/833-0690 or 414/887-0391. Over 300 sewing notions and accessories, serger threads and tools, interfacings and fabrics, and books and videos. Free color catalog.

National Thread & Supply, 695 Red Oak Rd., Stockbridge, GA 30281, 800/847-1001, ext. 1688; in GA, 404/389-9115. Name-brand sewing supplies and notions. Free catalog.

Sew-Fit Co., P.O. Box 397, Bedford Park, IL 60499, 800/547-4739. Sewing notions and accessories, cutting tables, cutting mats, special rulers, and T-squares. Free catalog.

Sewing Emporium, 1079 Third Ave., Chula Vista, CA 91910, 619/420-3490. Hard-to-find serger parts, notions, and accessories. Catalog, $4.95 (refundable with order).

Speed Stitch, 3113-D Broadpoint Dr., Harbor Heights, FL 33983, 800/874-4115. Machine-art kits and supplies, including all-purpose, decorative, and specialty serging threads, books, and accessories. Catalog, $3 (refundable with order).

Treadleart, 25834 Narbonne Ave., Lomita, CA 90717, 800/327-4222. Books, serging supplies, notions, decorative threads, and creative inspiration. Catalog, $3.

YLI Corporation, 482 N. Freedom Blvd., Provo, UT 84601, 800/854-1932 or 801/377-3900. Decorative, specialty, serger, and all-purpose threads, yarns, and ribbons. Catalog, $2.50.

Other Books by the Authors

Distinctive Serger Gifts & Crafts, by Naomi Baker and Tammy Young, Chilton Book Company, 1989, $14.95. The first book with one-of-a-kind serger projects using ingenious methods and upscale ideas.

Innovative Serging, by Gail Brown and Tammy Young, Chilton Book Company, 1989, $14.95. State-of-the-art techniques for overlock sewing.

Innovative Sewing, by Gail Brown and Tammy Young, Chilton Book Company, 1990, $14.95. The newest, best, and fastest sewing techniques.

Know Your baby lock, by Naomi Baker and Tammy Young, Chilton Book Company, 1990, $16.95. Ornamental serging techniques for all *baby lock* serger models.

Know Your Pfaff Hobbylock, by Naomi Baker and Tammy Young, Chilton Book Company, 1991, $16.95. Ornamental serging techniques for all *Hobbylock* serger models.

Know Your White Superlock, by Naomi Baker and Tammy Young, Chilton Book Company, 1991, $16.95. Ornamental serging techniques for all *Superlock* serger models.

Simply Serge Any Fabric, by Naomi Baker and Tammy Young, Chilton Book Company, 1990, $14.95. Tips and techniques for successfully serging all types of fabric.

Taming Decorative Serging, by Tammy Young, 1991, $14.95. A step-by-step workbook teaching special techniques for glamorous decorative serging.

Taming Your First Serger, by Lori Bottom, 1989, $14.95. A hands-on guide to basic serging skills in an easy-to-use, workbook format.

Look for these titles in your local stores, or write to: Tammy Young, 2269 Chestnut, Suite 269, San Francisco, CA 94123. To order, add $3.50 per book to the listed price for first-class postage and handling.

Handy Serging and Sewing Periodicals

Butterick Home Catalog, 161 Sixth Avenue, New York, NY 10013. Quarterly, $8.95/year.

The Creative Machine Newsletter, P.O. Box 2634, Menlo Park, CA 94026. Quarterly fanzine, $12/year.

McCall's Pattern Magazine, 230 Park Avenue, New York, NY 10169. Quarterly, $10/year.

Serger Update, P.O. Box 5026, Harlan, IA 51537. The only periodical devoted entirely to serging news and techniques. Monthly newsletter, $39/year.

Sewer's SourceLetter, CraftSource, 7509 7th Place SW, Seattle, WA 98106. Quarterly, $15/year.

Sewing Update, P.O. Box 5026, Harlan, IA 51537. Bimonthly newsletter, $19.50/year.

Sew News, Box 1790, Peoria, IL 61656. Monthly, $15.97/year.

Threads, The Taunton Press, Inc., 63 S. Main St., P.O. Box 5506, Newtown, CT 06470. Bimonthly magazine, $22/year.

Vogue Patterns Magazine, 161 Sixth Avenue, New York, NY 10013. Bimonthly, $12.95/year.

Index